RUSTIC SIMPLICITY

Scenes of Cottage Life in Nineteenth-Century British Art

Christiana Payne

Djanogly Art Gallery

The University of Nottingham Arts Centre.

26 September - 8 November 1998

———

Penlee House Gallery & Museum

Penzance.

25 November - 9 January 1999

ACKNOWLEDGEMENTS

Many people have given generously of their time and expertise to make this exhibition possible. I would particularly like to thank the following for their help with my research: Sarah Burns, Patsy Campbell, Robin Hamlyn, Christopher Lloyd, Anne Lyles, Eunice Martin, Lady Montagu Douglas Scott, Richard Ormond, Diane Perkins, Karen Sayer, Selina Skipwith, Kim Sloan, Helen Smailes, Sheena Stoddard, Linda Whiteley, Stephen Whittle, and Stephen Wildman. To the School of Humanities, Oxford Brookes University, I am grateful for study leave and a contribution towards expenses; my colleagues and students provided interest, enthusiasm and encouragement, more difficult to quantify but no less important to the realisation of the project. I am also grateful to David Bickerstaff for designing a beautiful catalogue.

Above all, I am indebted to the staff of the two galleries and to the many lenders, public and private, who have consented to part temporarily with their paintings, drawings and prints so that others can enjoy them. At Nottingham, Nicholas Alfrey, Tracey Isgar, Liz Reintjes, Neil Walker and Joanne Wright; and at Penzance, the late Hazel Burston and Jonathan Holmes, have all worked patiently on the many practical details involved in turning an exhibition idea into reality. It has been a real pleasure to work with them.

The catalogue is dedicated to Giles and Charlotte, with love.

First published in Great Britain in 1998 for the exhibition *Rustic Simplicity: Scenes of Cottage Life in Nineteenth-Century British Art* by the Djanogly Art Gallery, The University of Nottingham Arts Centre in association with Lund Humphries Publishers, Park House, 1 Russell Gardens, London NW11 9NN.
Financially supported by Oxford Brookes University.

Designed by David Bickerstaff
Printed by Goaters Limited, Nottingham.

Djanogly Art Gallery ISBN 1-900809-60-5
Lund Humphries ISBN 0 85331 747 X

Front Cover *Home and the Homeless* by Thomas Faed, (detail) (National Gallery of Scotland) [cat.no.16]

Back Cover *The Wife's Remonstrance* by James Cambell, (Birmingham Museum and Art Gallery) [cat.no.4]

In numbering the illustrations throughout the catalogue we have adopted the following convention. Exhibits are referred to as cat.nos., illustrative material and comparative illustrations in the introductory essay and catalogue are noted as figs.

CONTENTS

FOREWORD

Five years ago the Djanogly Art Gallery, in conjunction with the Yale Center for British Art, mounted *Toil and Plenty*, a highly successful exhibition which examined images of the agricultural landscape in English nineteenth-century art. That exhibition was expertly curated by the British Art scholar Dr Christiana Payne who was, even as it was being hung, already talking to us about another exhibition, one which would take the country folk out of the fields and place them in their domestic context. *Rustic Simplicity* is the realisation of that idea.

Rural genre painting was an extremely important and popular category of art in nineteenth-century Britain. The painters who specialised in it were very well known and respected by their contemporaries but have, latterly, been relatively neglected. In *Rustic Simplicity* Dr Payne redresses this state of affairs through her judicious selection of scenes of rural domestic life which she discusses both in an aesthetic and in a social historical context. Anyone who has read the novels of George Eliot or Thomas Hardy will recognise this world.

We are delighted to have had this opportunity to work again with Dr Payne and must record our thanks, both to her for all her hard work, and to her institution, Oxford Brookes University, for their willingness to support her research through their generous contribution to the production costs of the catalogue. The exhibition which tours to the Penlee House Gallery and Museum in Penzance at the end of the year will, I feel sure, be greatly enjoyed, both here and there, by a wide audience.

Joanne Wright

Director of Visual Art
University of Nottingham

RUSTIC SIMPLICITY
Scenes of Cottage Life in Nineteenth-Century British Art

Introduction

We forsake these sublime heights, around which the eagles soar, and the clouds cluster; we escape the unfathomable abyss into which genius has too often plunged headlong; and now, taking to the level and unambitious pathway of life, we greet the peasant smiling at the cottage door, we walk the humble streets of the rural village, enter the parson's parish school, or the labourer's dwelling, talk to the children and the mother neatly clad for church on Sunday morn, or join the circle of the cottar's Saturday night round the brightly-burning fire. Such has been the daily walk of many of our English artists, intent upon finding the poetry which lurks in our common humanity, ready to lend a heart to the joys and the sorrows of the sons of honest toil, willing to paint the simple annals of the poor, children of nature, dwellers among the hills, sojourners along the unbeaten solitary paths, around whose life the unsophisticated landscape of rural England prettily groups as a background...that truly English school of home sympathies and rustic simplicity, to which the foreign galleries of the International Exhibition afford little or no parallel...made sacred in the sphere of poetry by the writings of Crabbe and Wordsworth... (*Art Journal*, 1 June 1862, p.150)

The enthusiastic anonymous reviewer of the International Exhibition of 1862 identified rustic genre painting as the characteristic art of the English school.[1] He or she explicitly relates this type of painting to the poetry of George Crabbe and William Wordsworth, and describes its subject matter in language redolent of famous poems by Robert Burns and Thomas Gray, thus associating both painting and literature as emblems of national character and identity.[2] Amongst the genre painters discussed in the review are David Wilkie, Edward Bird, William Collins, Thomas Webster, and Thomas Faed. However, while the poets remain very well known, the artists (with the possible exception of Wilkie) are now known only to specialists. Despite their contemporary reputations, they have attracted relatively little attention in the twentieth century. Rustic genre paintings have been overlooked, or relegated to the basements of museums. The aim of this exhibition is to encourage a fresh look at these paintings, in order to try and understand why they exercised so much appeal in the time when they were painted, and to set them in the context of developments in nineteenth-century politics, social reform and artistic theory.

Rustic genre painting is a part of the wider category of genre painting (paintings of everyday life), the importance of which in the development of Victorian art has long been recognised. Famous nineteenth-century genre paintings include the crowd scenes of William Powell Frith, such as *Derby Day* (1856-8, Tate Gallery), illustrations from literature or history, and commentaries on modern life problems such as Augustus Egg's trilogy, *Past and Present* (1858, Tate Gallery). It was the rustic genre scenes of Wilkie, however, that began the fashion for genre in nineteenth-century Britain, and rustic genre continued to attract specialists, such as Thomas Webster and Thomas Faed, until the 1860s and 1870s. Unlike the paintings of Frith and Egg, rustic genre focussed on the poor people of the countryside: in some senses it was less "modern" than urban genre painting, but it dealt with important issues which aroused much concern in the period. Paintings of cottage interiors could demonstrate the virtues and good character of the rural poor - and by extension, of the nation as a whole. Depictions of "village politicians" and of village schools were related to debates about the extension of the suffrage and the education of the working classes, in town as well as country. The poetic legacy, of Gray, Crabbe, Burns, Wordsworth and others, had prepared the ground for a widespread interest in, and sympathy for, the "joys and sorrows" of rustic life, amongst those who went to exhibitions and bought paintings.

If the subjects chosen by rustic genre painters were often taken from poetry, the ways in which they were treated had more in common with novels and plays. Like nineteenth-century novels, these paintings incorporate careful characterisation; a psychological study of relationships between different characters; pathos or humour; closely-observed passages of description, involving not simply the outlines of objects but the subtleties of light and shade, colour and reflection. The novels of Sir Walter Scott, George Eliot and Thomas Hardy, all of whom were deeply interested in the painting of their time, offer particularly close parallels. It is instructive to read, for example, George Eliot's description of the Poyser household at Hall Farm in *Adam Bede* (1859) with rustic genre painting in mind. She begins with the building and its furnishings: the glittering brass candlesticks, polished oak table and pewter dishes indicate the cleanliness of the house:

> Everything was looking at its brightest at this moment, for the sun shone right on the pewter dishes, and from their reflecting surfaces pleasant jets of light were thrown on mellow oak and bright brass - and on a still pleasanter object than these; for some of the rays fell on Dinah's finely-moulded cheek, and lit up her pale red hair to auburn, as she bent over the heavy household linen which she was mending for her aunt.

From the objects in the room, the description moves seamlessly to an analysis of the main characters, Dinah and her aunt: their features and activities indicate their personalities, as does their dress. Mrs Poyser's plain cap and gown, for example, tell us that "there was no weakness of which she was less tolerant than feminine vanity"; Eliot notes "the contrast between her (Mrs Poyser's) keenness and Dinah's seraphic gentleness of expression". Before the characters have opened their mouths the viewer is made aware of their personalities, by means of the same kind of visual clues that were employed by the rustic genre painters of the time. Even the slow pace of this descriptive passage, which takes up four pages before the dialogue begins, is comparable to the time needed for the viewer to appreciate all the details of a rustic genre painting.[3]

There are close links, too, with the art of the dramatist. Stage-like settings and exaggerated gestures were adopted because they made the story and characters easier to read, following the example of William Hogarth, whose "modern moral subjects" in the mid-eighteenth century had been deliberately conceived like the scenes in a play. As Martin Meisel has shown, there were particularly close links with the theatre in the work of David Wilkie. Wilkie was an enthusiastic theatre-goer, who probably picked up many of his ideas for subjects and compositions from the contemporary stage. In the 1830s, a number of plays used well-known paintings by him to create readily recognisable *tableaux vivants* with which to open or close their acts: *The Village Politicians* and *Distraining for Rent* (cats.45,47) were both used in this way. The stage directions for the original production of Douglas Jerrold's *Rent Day* (1832) end the first act with the main character, Martin Heywood, crying out "God help us! God help us! (buries his face in his hands. The other characters so arrange themselves as to represent WILKIE'S Picture of 'DISTRAINING FOR RENT')".[4] Wilkie attended a performance, and wrote to Jerrold to express his thanks and approval.[5] The links of genre painting with poetry, novels and plays gave the contemporary viewer levels of resonance and recognition which we can hardly reconstruct today, especially as much of the literature concerned is ephemeral. The poetry and short stories published in the many nineteenth-century periodicals, as well as details of play performances which have left no written record, must all have helped to shape the viewer's responses to the paintings. These literary parallels are all the more relevant because genre painting, like a novel or a play, is a study of the human condition, encompassing the ages of man and the joys and sorrows of life, including childhood, maturity, old age, celebration, misfortune, learning, crime, family affection, religious belief, involving situations that each viewer could apply to their own experience: Shakespeare's tag "one touch of nature makes the whole world kin" was especially popular with Victorian artists and critics.[6]

Like the writer quoted at the start of this Introduction, many nineteenth-century viewers would have regarded rustic genre paintings as illustrations of "the poetry which lurks in our common humanity". The twentieth-century historian, however, cannot help being conscious of the issue of class in this valuation. Those who looked at the paintings and wrote about them were, on the whole, middle class and predominantly urban; those whose lives were represented in them were the rural working class - "the sons of honest toil".[7] This is explained partly by the widespread belief, expressed succinctly by Wordsworth, that "low and rustic life" was the place where the human passions were to be seen in their purest form, whereas sophisticated society had developed polite conventions which had the effect of concealing the feelings and distorting human relationships (see below, p.23). But the class issue means that these paintings embody beliefs, not just about humanity in general, but also, more specifically, about the characteristics and desirable virtues of the rural poor and, by implication, of the working class in town as well as country.

This is an obstacle to their appreciation in the twentieth century, as it was to some critics in the mid and late nineteenth century. Rural poverty existed within a framework of paternalism and deference, already coming to be seen as old-fashioned and patronising in the mid-nineteenth century, hopelessly outmoded now. In paintings, rural families are presented as they might appear to the benevolent visitor from the "big house": hardworking, respectable, but ready to be grateful for a gift of coal or blankets. Some paintings, like the now-notorious *Rustic Civility* by William Collins (cat.7), make this explicit: the ragged children hold open the gate for the squire on horseback, whose shadow falls across the foreground; the boy, in the words of a contemporary critic, "puts his hand to where his hat should be, and makes an obeisance with his looks".[8] The *Art Journal* reviewer's evocation of artists walking into the parish school or the labourer's dwelling may be intended to suggest sympathy, but reads to us as patronising condescension. Furthermore, many rustic genre paintings depict a set of virtues - including frugality, contentment and industriousness - whose widespread adoption by the poor would make life easier for the rich. These desirable virtues were promoted by a large number of texts and images in this period, many of which were self-consciously didactic in their tone and function.[9]

Since the mid-nineteenth century, then, changes in political attitudes have made it difficult to judge rustic genre paintings fairly. They have also suffered from changes in artistic priorities: new forms of realism in the mid and later nineteenth century put the emphasis on dirt, squalor and disease - areas which many rustic genre paintings play down or ignore. The modernist stress on originality also militates against the appreciation of paintings which are so clearly part of a tradition, stretching back to seventeenth-century Dutch genre painting. In the late nineteenth century, narrative painting went out of fashion, and the "novelistic" qualities that the rustic genre painters worked so hard to achieve came to seem inferior in comparison to formal values. Finally, a reaction against sentimentality meant that another characteristic of these paintings, so much admired in their time, was devalued: their perceived ability to stimulate benevolent feelings in the observer towards his or her fellow men and women.

Even at the date of the opening quotation, 1862, the critical reaction against rustic genre painting, which has laid the foundation for twentieth-century judgments of it, was well advanced. Many of the indictments of this type of painting are eminently quotable, a tempting corrective to the complacency of writers like the *Art Journal* critic. However, to adopt these attitudes uncritically lays us open, in our turn, to the charge of complacency: there is a danger that we will too readily regard the Victorians as patronising and self-deluding in order to confirm our belief that we have made moral progress since their time. While accepting that complete objectivity is impossible, this introductory essay aims to adopt a balanced approach, allowing both positive and negative appraisals of rustic genre painting to be considered. The first chapter analyses selected paintings in depth, to demonstrate the qualities found by contemporaries in these paintings. We then move on to the visual sources used by nineteenth-century rustic genre painters, showing that they could be both selective and creative in their approach to the tradition. Chapters Three and Four consider the themes of cottage genre, both reassuring and controversial, in relation to the social and political issues of the time. Chapter Five looks at the consumers of rustic genre, ranging from aristocratic connoisseurs of fine paintings to the poor exhibition-goers who, it was hoped, would be morally improved by their experience of art. Finally, in Chapter Six, we return to those influential critics of rustic genre, and to some of the historical circumstances which made such paintings the object of satire and disdain.

CHAPTER ONE
Character, Sentiment and Truth: the Qualities of Rustic Genre Painting

There is a fine moral tone in the works of Wilkie, and their circulation among all classes of the community cannot fail of producing, together with a taste for art, refining and humanizing influences. They deal with the common things of life, and, with subtle penetration, but no unkindly feeling, satirize our common infirmities and foibles, detect and exhibit the humorous and ridiculous, and throw an interest over the simple and joyous amusements of domestic life...While the admirer of [Wilkie's] genius gazes with delight on the results of consummate art and original powers...his feelings are drawn out; he sees what he had never before remarked; familiar things assume also a more beautiful aspect, and he becomes, in a measure, more gentle, refined, and charitable in his tastes and feelings. (Anon., *The Wilkie Gallery*, 1851)

The qualities looked for by critics in nineteenth-century rustic genre paintings can be summed up in three words: character, sentiment and truth.[10] Artists were expected to depict convincing figures, whose actions, facial expressions, and clothing were consistent with their character. The painting was meant to stimulate feeling, and feeling of the right sort: humour, pathos, but above all sympathy and benevolence. Finally, it should demonstrate truth to nature, not only in the figures, but also in the setting, whether this was a cottage interior or a landscape. Artists used a variety of methods to achieve these results. Some made many preparatory drawings, working on the expression of individual figures or on the relationships of people in groups; others painted directly onto the panel or canvas. Some studied models in the studio in London, others settled in the country and deliberately sought out authentic rural labourers for their figures. An analysis of examples chosen from different periods in the nineteenth-century will show how their methods varied, and how these demands were satisfied.

The most important British rustic genre painter of the nineteenth century was Sir David Wilkie. He was born in Scotland, but came to England in 1805, where he soon achieved fame with his *Village Politicians* (cat.45), exhibited at the Royal Academy in 1806. His earliest paintings were very close in style to those of the seventeenth-century Flemish artist, David Teniers, and his subject matter was often Scottish genre, although based on London models or, for expression, studies of his own face in a mirror. He made many drawings, following, at least from around 1809, the traditional Italian practice (associated with history painting rather than genre painting) of doing compositional sketches followed by studies of individual figures from life.[11] Wilkie's *Penny Wedding* (cat.48) dates from a transitional point in his career, when he was moving from a minutely detailed to a looser style, and when the study of Teniers was being replaced by

the deeper chiaroscuro of Rembrandt and a lightness and elegance in the figures which owes much to Watteau. A watercolour study (cat.52) shows that he refined the composition, cutting down the numbers of dancers, making the composition easier to read, although perhaps more contrived and less logical. The setting of the dance is lovingly delineated, with multifarious objects piled up on shelves and on top of the cupboard. A spinning wheel and a saddle can be made out in the shadows on the right, and there are plates, buckets and other utensils all around the room, emblems of hardworking rustic life, temporarily put aside for the festivities. In the foreground there is a group of finely painted objects, apparently selected, like the items in a still life painting, for their contrasts of colour and texture, and for effects of transparency and reflection.

The bridal couple steps forward on the left, the wife tentative, the husband protective. Behind them, another couple provides amusement for the old lady carrying food and the young girl on the extreme right. The expressions of this couple were carefully studied in a separate drawing (cat.51): the girl looks away in feigned indifference, the man's face is full of mischievous anticipation. The humour of the situation is one that viewers could relate to their own experience: the bashfulness of young love, the delights of gentle teasing. In other characters the humour perceived by a middle-class critic was more patronising and class-based, as in this comment in an article written in 1842:

The auld wives, as usual, bear off the bell. One, occupied in that kind of stationary dancing practised by common people, who lift their legs as a steam-engine its pump-rods parallel to each other, always from the same spots, is laughter for a twelvemonth: - her visage so full of self-complaisance, her clumsiness so buoyant with good humour![12]

Characters are differentiated according to their rank in life: the old lady on the extreme right, who is accompanied by a man in a wig, is reticent and dignified, in contrast both to the exuberance of the dancing woman and to the unabashed curiosity of the old lady looking at the young couple on the left. Thus, people behave according to their character and relate to one another in ways that the viewer can understand, appealing both to ideas about universal human nature and to contemporary perceptions of class differences. Even the dogs suggest class and character differences, a device that was common in poems and novels as well as in painting.[13]

Many painters learnt from Wilkie's example, constructing stage-like settings on which groups of figures were arranged, contrasting in character and action. William Mulready's *The Last In* (cat.31) depicts a schoolroom, into which a boy has entered late; the schoolmaster bows in mock politeness, but the boy's nervous look tells us that he is aware that politeness will soon give way to harsh sarcasm and punishment. Once again, a dog provides a commentary on the human drama (although it seems incongruous in the schoolroom setting). The reactions of his schoolmates are a study in character: the boys outside wait to see how their companion is treated; two girls on the right strain to see the spectacle. Only the girl in white shows any compassion for the boy, while, in front of her, other boys, one of whom has already been punished, concentrate on their work, not daring to look up. A contemporary critic wrote "the piteous look of the culprit is truly heart-rending, and the hardened indifference of some of his schoolfellows most provoking. Others appear as if they would fain deprecate the approaching storm".[14] As in Wilkie's painting, the setting is carefully painted and important to the meaning of the picture: the heavy locks on the door contrast with the idyllic landscape seen through the open window, emphasizing the prison-like effect of the shackled boy in the foreground. Mulready's subject is a variation on a theme made popular by the seventeenth-century Dutch artist, Jan Steen, but his composition and colour reveal his study of the Italian Renaissance masters, and particularly of Raphael's fresco *The School at Athens*, which he would have known from reproductions. Like his Italian predecessors, he made many drawings, and for some of his genre scenes, including this one, he made cartoons, as if he were a history painter (cats.33,34). Thus, the harmonious arrangement of his figures was carefully worked out.

In contrast to the tradition established by Wilkie and his successors, the Pre-Raphaelites and their associates painted directly from nature, choosing authentic peasants for their models. This was in keeping with the general aims of the Pre-Raphaelite Brotherhood, founded in 1848, which set out to purify contemporary painting by returning to the bright colours and close study of nature which they admired in the early Renaissance masters. James Campbell's painting of a poacher and his family, *The Wife's Remonstrance* (cat.4) was for a long time attributed to John Everett Millais, who also started a picture of this theme, which he never finished.[15] Campbell's poacher has patched trousers, and features that are more plebeian than those of earlier genre painting; his wife's hands and arms are strong and show the marks of labour, in contrast to the softness and whiteness that were traditional in previous depictions of the working class. A contemporary review, however, judges the painting in terms of its characterisation and depiction of emotion; its emphasis is surprising, and shows the strength of the genre painting tradition and the expectations it set up for the viewer.

> The Wife's Remonstrance...showed a wife entreating a ruffian poacher to abandon that way of life; there was a fine, rude, eloquent passion on her care-worn and squalid face that remains in one's memory with singular force; the husband, also, was finely conceived - a hard-hearted, stupid brute, whose shame covered itself with indignation at his partner's words to which he could not refuse conviction, although obstinate anger kept him on his old vile course.[16]

Compared to the work of Wilkie and Mulready, the figures in Pre-Raphaelite genre paintings are stiffer, their expressions harder to read (partly because their methods involved posing models for hours at a time); documentary truth was achieved at the expense of fluid narrative. The final effect is less contrived, and in a sense more realistic, although an admirer of Wilkie might judge that the reduction in fluency and legibility is a defect rather than an improvement.

In the same period, a group of Scottish painters, of whom the most famous was Thomas Faed, continued Wilkie's methods. Faed, like Wilkie, settled in London and exhibited scenes of Scottish life, increasingly based on his memories of Scotland, rather than on direct experience. *Home and the Homeless* (cat.16) draws on Wilkie's *Blind Fiddler* (fig.1) in contrasting a self-sufficient cottage family with a family who are in need of their charity: in this case, a widow and her two children (with the dogs, once again, providing a parallel to the human figures). The contrast between the faces of the two mothers - the one plump, healthy and happy, the other drawn, fearful and haunted - is striking, and was noted by contemporary critics. One wrote "the smiling mother eyes this group (her husband and children) with an unaffected pride that wins the heart at once. But, while we look at the bright, there is also the dark side of the picture...In our estimation the grand point of the picture is the utter desolation of that widowed mother's face:..we only bid the spectator read for himself the unutterable things her face reveals."[17] The painting stimulated feelings of sympathy - and, in particular, the sympathy of the well-off for the destitute poor, the basis of charity and philanthropy. The setting is delineated with great precision: the view of mountains through the tiny window, the signs of wear and repair on the cupboard behind the happy mother, the mixture of earth, stone and brick in the floor, all suggest observation of actual cottages in the remoter parts of the British Isles. The ill-fitting clothes (presumably second-hand) of the child who stands at the table are further evidence of an attempt at documentary realism similar to that of the Pre-Raphaelites.

Fig.1 Sir David Wilkie, *The Blind Fiddler*,1806
Oil on Panel, 57.8 x 79.4 cm, © Tate Gallery, London 1998

While Faed was exhibiting scenes of Scottish peasant life, a group of painters known as the Cranbrook Colony were producing pictures of cottage interiors in Kent. Thomas Webster, Frederick Daniel Hardy and a number of other painters took up residence in the large village of Cranbrook in Kent in the 1840s and 1850s. Their pictures were based on their study of actual cottages, and local inhabitants posed for them. However, this did not guarantee documentary accuracy: their interiors are usually spacious, well-kept and appealing, the figures in them neat and prosperous. In some paintings by Hardy, such as *Preparing for Dinner* (cat.22), the concentration on balanced, almost geometric compositions, harmonies of colour and the beauties of texture in old cottages,

become more important than character and narrative. The old brick of the walls and floor, the play of light on the surfaces, seize the attention as much, if not more than, the static, self-absorbed figures. Their expressions and character are hard to read, beyond a sense of concentration and submissive devotion to their mundane domestic tasks. *The Dismayed Artist* (cat.24) is different: here, a painter arrives to work on his study of a cottage interior, only to find that its occupants are whitewashing the ancient features that he has been depicting with such loving care. As the painting indicates, this group of artists painted directly from nature without making preliminary drawings.

Later in the century, British genre painters were affected by developments on the Continent. Another group of artists, the Newlyn School, settled in the fishing village of Newlyn, in Cornwall, and, like the Cranbrook artists, made use of local models and interiors to give authenticity to their work. However, following the example of French artists like Jules Bastien-Lepage and, later, the Impressionists, they adopted apparently haphazard compositions, unusual viewpoints, lighter colours and a sketchier technique. Elizabeth Forbes's *School is Out* (cat.20) is a depiction of a schoolroom which makes earlier examples look staged and contrived. The children are shown in the schoolroom in the neighbouring village of Paul; according to oral tradition, they were portraits of actual children in the school at the time. Their costumes and school books are those of the period. Character and sentiment have not disappeared entirely, however: the boy rubbing his eyes on the left, and the group of girls looking at him, one sympathetic, the others laughing, represent a situation that is not unlike the one shown in Mulready's *The Last In*.

Nineteenth-century critics looked at these paintings in distinctive ways, judging them according to the feelings they evoked as well as their documentary accuracy. In many cases, they studied them very closely, picking up narrative clues, analogous to those used by the novelists of the time, which are often lost on the twentieth-century viewer. Above all they looked for convincing characters, expressions and situations, which would give evidence of the artist's insight into human nature (and often, into human nature as displayed in a particular class). This was important to them because of the "refining and humanizing influences" which were thought to be produced by art in general, and by rustic genre in particular: it was widely believed that, as the anonymous author of the letterpress to *The Wilkie Gallery* put it, people could become "more gentle, refined, and charitable" by looking at such paintings.

CHAPTER TWO
Tradition and Mutation: the Artistic Sources for Nineteenth-Century British Genre Painting

Our English and Scotch art in this department has certainly always been more refined than its kindred Dutch. Instead of placing our characters in a dirty back-kitchen wallowing in mire, with the pigs as playmates, we have an eye to comfort and cleanliness, sweep the floor, put the furniture in order, dress the household in well-to-do fashion, make them thrifty, tidy people, who work hard during the week and go to church on Sundays. (Anon., "The Royal Academy and other Exhibitions", *Blackwood's Edinburgh Magazine*, July 1860, p.70)

Rustic genre paintings were not, of course, simply reflections of contemporary life. They belong to a long artistic tradition, stretching back to the seventeenth century. Pictures of everyday life first became well established in the art of the Netherlands in the seventeenth century. David Teniers and Adriaen Brouwer painted tavern scenes and scenes of merrymaking; Adriaen van Ostade depicted humble cottage interiors; Jan Steen painted schoolrooms and poor families saying grace; Nicolaes Maes and Pieter de Hooch depicted more prosperous, middle-class families, often focussing on housewives and children in tidy, well-scrubbed rooms.[18] Many of the favourite subjects of the nineteenth-century painters are clearly derived from this tradition. However, the artists, as critics of the time were keen to point out, made significant adaptations to the tradition (and also to their borrowings from eighteenth-century sources), which are very revealing of the different values of nineteenth-century British society.

Dutch and Flemish painters were working in England in the seventeenth century and even before then, so the tradition of Dutch genre was well known in Britain. In the late eighteenth century, with the dispersal of important French collections as a result of revolution and war, there was a surge of interest in this school of painting. Notable collections were formed in early nineteenth-century Britain which included many genre paintings, and in several cases the collectors were also patrons of modern British art, men like the Marquis of Stafford, Sir George Beaumont, the Duke of Wellington and Sir Robert Peel.[19] In 1815 the first exhibition of Old Masters held by the British Institution was devoted to Dutch and Flemish painting, and in 1829 John Smith began publishing a nine-volume catalogue raisonné of the works of Dutch, Flemish and French painters.[20] Academic theory regarded genre painting as of lower status than history painting, and the Dutch School as inferior to the Italian because it dealt with common nature rather than ideal beauty; nevertheless, there was widespread admiration for the remarkable skill displayed by the Dutch painters in the depiction of objects, skills which their modern British counterparts vied to emulate.

In many respects, seventeenth-century Holland was comparable to nineteenth-century Britain, and rustic genre painting served similar purposes in both cultures. Protestantism, a widening market for art, and a regard for education, charity and family life produced a similar focus in painting on, for example, happy families saying grace, or mothers instructing their children. However, nineteenth-century British writers on art were keen to point out the ways in which, they felt, the British painters had improved on their predecessors. Artists were praised for avoiding the more revolting aspects of Dutch and Flemish art, and for giving their works a moral purpose, along with a greater emphasis on beauty, character and narrative. Wilkie's biographer, Allan Cunningham, wrote that he did not "save in one or two groups, stumble into the dirty Dutch path to reputation, and wallow in a mire unworthy of being painted".[21] In 1810, an anonymous critic claimed that the Dutch "transferred to their canvas...the very identity of the objects they saw, without any improvement from the standards of ideal beauty, and without infusing into them any distinct sentiment of character and action", but the English school "has superadded humour and sentiment to figure, and a certain definite action, or, what we might call in poetry a MINOR FABLE, to the justness of form".[22] Such arguments helped to exalt the status of genre painting, making it seem more like history painting.

Wilkie's *Village Politicians* (cat.45) made a great impact when it was exhibited in 1806, and all who saw it noted the similarities with Teniers. It is not difficult to find sources for the composition and the still life details in Teniers and in Brouwer; however, compared to these earlier artists, Wilkie's figures have more individuality and display a wider range of emotions.

Fig.2 David Teniers the Younger, *Boors Carousing*, 1644.
Oil on Copper, 36 x 50.2 cm. Reproduced by Permission of the Trustees of
the Wallace Collection, London.

Fig.3 Jan Steen, *A School for Boys and Girls*, ca. 1670.
Oil on Canvas, 81.7 x 108.6 cm. National Gallery of Scotland

Fig.4 Sir David Wilkie, The *Village School*, 1820-22.
Oil on Panel, 101.6 x 152.4cm. Private Collection.

Lindsay Errington has stressed its originality as "a study of group psychology in action".[23] If we compare the Wilkie with Teniers' *Boors Carousing* (fig.2), for example, the parallels in the composition, lighting, and setting are very obvious. However, while Teniers' characters smoke or play cards, watch others or indulge in reverie, Wilkie's are engaged in political debate. Some of his characters are like the stereotypical rustic boors of earlier art, but these are contrasted with figures who look more intelligent and thoughtful, like the two foreground figures at the table in *The Village Politicians*. Contemporary critics noted this as proof of Wilkie's superiority to Teniers; in 1806 Lord Mulgrave told Joseph Farington that "he believed Wilkie would go beyond Teniers, Ostade & all who had preceded him, as he not only gave exquisitely the ordinary expressions of the human countenance but those of thought and abstraction"; by contrast, thought Humphrey Repton, Teniers rarely showed any passion except the progress of intoxication.[24]

Certain aspects of earlier genre painting were deliberately avoided by the nineteenth-century painters. Many seventeenth-century genre paintings employ sexual symbolism and innuendo; others poke fun at professional men, particularly doctors, lawyers and schoolmasters. In an age of popular revolutions, the need to encourage respect for figures of authority meant that the anarchic and subversive features of the earlier tradition were played down; and evangelical prudishness ensured that nineteenth-century genre was more "decorous" than its sources. Paintings of village schools, for example, draw on Dutch precedents, but with very different results. In Jan Steen's *A School for Boys and Girls* (fig.3; probably exhibited in the British Institution's exhibition of Dutch and Flemish paintings in 1815),[25] the schoolroom is dark and untidy, the master inattentive and the pupils, with only one or two exceptions, have no desire to learn. Wilkie's unfinished *The Village School* (fig.4) is similar in composition, but his schoolroom is bright and well-ordered, and a sizable group of children are reciting their lessons, while distractions are confined to the periphery. In place of anarchy and disorder, then, Wilkie provides a reassuring depiction of well-disciplined children and kindly teachers. This tradition was carried on later in the nineteenth-century by Sir George Harvey and Thomas Faed (cats.25,15). The nineteenth-century paintings can be closely related to current debates over education which, it was thought, would improve social harmony by making the working class more disciplined and respectful.

Similarly, the family groups in cottage interiors by

Adriaen van Ostade stimulated British artists to depict similar subjects, but the latter adapted their sources to show cottages that were neater and more modern, with figures which looked more prosperous in their clothing and demeanour. In the 1850s, the paintings of the Cranbrook Colony depicted cottage interiors, but with well-scrubbed floors, bright colours and a careful differentiation of textures which recalls the middle-class interiors of de Hooch or Vermeer rather than the more subdued colouring of Dutch and Flemish peasant genre proper. Frederick Daniel Hardy's *Preparing for Dinner* (cat.22), for example, takes as its model de Hooch's *A Woman Peeling Apples* (fig.5), which was sold in London in 1848, but transposes the mother and child group from a prosperous, bourgeois interior to a rustic cottage, altering their clothing and demeanour accordingly. De Hooch's mother and child sit in the corner of a room with a grand fireplace and a tiled floor; they wear expensive fabrics, such as the mother's fur-lined jacket. Hardy's are placed in a kitchen with a brick floor and exposed brick walls, and their clothes are simple and utilitarian. The uses made by British artists of their Dutch sources strongly suggest a belief in moral progress, as a result of which the virtues formerly practised by the middle class have percolated down to a lower social level.

British painters of genre took many of their subjects from the earlier tradition, but they also added new ones, prompted by specific social conditions which had not existed in seventeenth-century Holland. The most important examples of these are emigration scenes, poaching scenes and depictions of people going to the village church (cats.1,4,8,17,18,21,37,40). Even when they chose time-honoured subjects, the emphasis was different: positive recommendations to virtue were much preferred to warnings against vice. As a result, there are many more paintings of happy families in well-kept cottage interiors in the art of nineteenth-century Britain than in the art of seventeenth-century Holland, and far fewer of the "sinful" subjects, such as portrayals of peasants in alehouses. Nineteenth-century writers on art were conscious of the dangers of depicting bad behaviour in paintings which would be seen by the lower classes and possibly emulated by them. The emphasis, therefore, was on demonstrating the exemplary and the commendable: "thrifty, tidy people who work hard during the week and go to church on Sundays".

Seventeenth-century Dutch and Flemish genre painting had been admired by eighteenth-century artists in both Britain and France: the modifications made to the tradition by William Hogarth and Jean-Baptiste Greuze, in particular, were important precedents for British nineteenth-century genre painters. The French painter, Greuze, developed a new type of genre painting in which a deliberate attempt is made to stir the emotions of the spectator. A flourishing market in prints ensured that French art became well known in England in the later eighteenth century, although recurrent wars between the two countries led to a reluctance to acknowledge any direct influence, especially in the early years of the nineteenth century. Greuze made his name with paintings that reflected the literary and philosophical movement known as "sensibilité": this held that the spontaneous display of emotion both proved, and developed virtue. To be moved to tears, whether at the theatre or in front of a painting, was a sign of a good character (and this applied as much to men as to women).[26] Greuze's paintings inspired a degree of emotional identification in the critics, above all in the writings of Denis Diderot, who admired Greuze because his works were moving, and because they preached good morality: "to render virtue agreeable, vice odious, to call attention to the ridiculous, this is the project of any honourable man who takes up the pen, the brush or the chisel."[27] Sensibility had a profound impact on art and literature in Britain as well as in France, and these qualities were to be found valuable by British critics in the paintings of Wilkie, Webster and their contemporaries.

Fig.5 Pieter de Hooch, *A Woman Peeling Apples*, ca. 1663. Oil on Canvas, 67.1 x 54.7 cm. Reproduced by Permission of the Trustees of the Wallace Collection, London.

Greuze's first genre painting, *La Lecture de la Bible (Reading the Bible)* (fig.6), exhibited at the Paris salon in 1755, showed a father reading the Bible to his assembled family, with the implication that this is a weekly event. The painting became the prototype for British paintings of the same theme, whose titles emphasize the regularity of the custom (cat.5). Wilkie's *The Cotter's Saturday Night* (cat.49) looks very different from Greuze's painting, but includes details which are not in its literary source (the poem by Robert Burns) and which might have been suggested by the Greuze; in each painting a small child, presumably too young to understand the reading, plays with an animal. Webster's *Sunday Evening* (fig.7) has closer visual similarities, including the placement of the old man on the left and the boy reading over his father's shoulder. But there are also striking differences; Webster's figures are altogether neater, both in their posture and their dress, just as his composition is more ordered and his cottage interior more spacious. The father and mother (or servant) in Greuze's painting look old enough to be the grandparents (perhaps reflecting Greuze's own knowledge of the rapid ageing brought about by the toil and privations of peasant life), but Webster clearly shows three generations, all equally hale and hearty. The British painting, therefore, modifies its probable source to emphasize the "respectable" virtues and relative prosperity of the English peasantry.

Greuze's paintings were well known in Britain through prints. In 1837 the volume devoted by John Smith to French painting includes only three artists: Claude, Poussin and Greuze. In his catalogue, he discusses each of Greuze's genre paintings in detail, praising them as "excellent."[28] He describes *L'Accordée de Village (The Village Bride)* (fig.8) as a "superlative production".[29] This painting develops the theme of the simple virtues of peasant life: it shows the father of the bride giving the dowry to his prospective son-in-law, recorded by a notary, a procedure which, for French Catholics, was the preliminary to the religious ceremony of marriage. The figures are arranged as in a *tableau vivant*, in an ordered, carefully balanced composition which moves from the seated figures on the outside of the group to those standing in the centre, creating semicircles both in height and in depth. This painting seems to have offered a particularly useful lesson to British artists who wished to compose a large group of figures in a rustic setting. When Wilkie went to Paris in 1814, he presumably saw *L'Accordée de Village* in the Louvre, yet he makes no mention of it in his letters or journal. His general

Fig.6 Jean-Baptiste Greuze, *La Lecture de la Bible*, 1753. Oil on Canvas, 80 x 64cm. Private Collection

Fig.7 Thomas Webster, *Sunday Evening*, 1858. Oil on Canvas, 58.4 x 91.4cm. William H. Proby Esq. Photograph Courtauld Institute of Art

Fig.8 Jean-Baptiste Greuze, *L'Accordée de Village*, 1761. Oil on Canvas, 92 x 117cm. Musée du Louvre

remarks about French painting are disparaging, perhaps influenced by patriotic feeling at the apparent conclusion of many years of war between the two countries.[30] This is all the more remarkable since Wilkie's *Blind Fiddler* of 1806 (fig.1) is strikingly similar in composition to *L'Accordée de Village*. The transition from seated to standing figures, the girl leaning on the back of a chair on the right, and the careful differentiation between characters all suggest a knowledge of Greuze's composition. *Distraining for Rent* (cat.47), which Wilkie had started before his visit to France and which he completed on his return, again takes the general composition of *L'Accordée* and incorporates specific borrowings, such as the two women on the far left and the open cupboard. In this case, the similarities are so close, because of the presence of the lawyer in Wilkie's painting, and the man offering money in the centre, that Wilkie may have intended an ironic contrast with the French painting; Greuze's picture shows the beneficial influence of the law in humble family life, Wilkie shows how it can be used to disrupt and destroy.

The composition of *L'Accordée de Village* was also adapted by Thomas Faed, in *Sunday in the Backwoods* (cat.17). Here, a father reads the Bible to his family, who are gathered round in a semicircle, with a seated woman on the left in much the same position as the mother in Greuze's painting. But, whereas Greuze's family represents a settled life, occupying a house lived in, presumably, by their parents and grandparents, Faed's is far from home and the young woman to left of centre is ill, evoking thoughts of the sad effects of emigration. Greuze's peasants have to deal only with the sadnesses of universal family life - children growing up and moving away from home - but in the nineteenth-century British paintings there are social pressures as well. Peasants are thrown out of their homes by cruel landlords, or they are forced to start a new life far from home. The work of Greuze set an important precedent for paintings of peasant life which celebrated humble virtues, incorporating narrative, sentiment and differentiation between characters. Indeed, all the qualities which nineteenth-century critics said British painters had added to the model established by Dutch and Flemish genre actually had earlier manifestations in the work of Greuze.

Another important precedent for nineteenth-century genre - and one that was easier to acknowledge on patriotic grounds - was the work of Hogarth. While Hogarth's aim, like Diderot's, was to recommend virtue and discourage vice, his characters are, more often than not, sinners whose lives illustrate the consequences of vice rather than the rewards of virtue (such as the rake and the harlot who were the stars of two of his most famous series of "modern moral subjects"). The worst characters in Hogarth's series are generally the rich rather than the poor, and professional men who exploit their customers, including doctors, lawyers and clergymen. Conservative critics were, therefore, cautious in recommending Hogarth as a model for emulation. In 1811 the critic of the *Morning Post* wrote that Hogarth's style and composition could not be proposed as models for imitation; but he had first discovered the mine, it was the business of others to refine and polish the ore.[31]

Industry and Idleness (1747) was probably the series which had most relevance for rural genre painting, since it dealt with vice and virtue in humble life - although, like all Hogarth's work, its setting was self-consciously urban. This contrasts the fortunes of two apprentices, who begin by working for the same master: the idle apprentice neglects his work, falls in with bad company, takes to crime and dies on the gallows; the industrious apprentice, meanwhile, marries his master's daughter and becomes Lord Mayor of London. Hogarth hoped that this series would be bought by those who had most to learn from it, that is, by apprentices. The whole set of engravings was too expensive for this purpose, but the artist was pleased to hear that masters gave sets to their apprentices as Christmas presents; a contemporary noted that all ranks of people discussed the prints outside print shops.[32] The didactic purpose of this series, and the deliberate attempt to use it to influence the behaviour of the working class, were both important precedents for the nineteenth century.

Fig.9 Edward Bird, *The Poacher's Reprieve*, 1813.
Oil on Panel, 45.1 x 60 cm. Guildhall Art Gallery.Corporation of London.

Hogarth's influence is most obvious in nineteenth-century paintings which contrast vice and virtue in a pair of images, or else illustrate the rise or fall of a character in a series of pictures. The sins of the idle apprentice - whoring and thieving - are often transmuted, in a rural setting, to poaching. In 1837 Edward Prentis exhibited a pair of paintings entitled "*Fruits of Idleness* - a wounded poacher, with his terrified family - and *Fruits of Industry*, a cottage dinner".[33] Edward Bird's series of six paintings, exhibited in 1813, illustrating the fall and rehabilitation of a poacher is also clearly indebted to Hogarth. It is, however, entirely symptomatic of the contrast between Hogarth's time and Bird's that Bird's poacher is saved through the intervention of a kindly clergyman. In the Royal Academy catalogue, the title of the sixth in the series (fig.9) was given as follows:

The poacher released from his imprisonment, during which he has been attended through a severe fit of illness by his amiable wife, whose kind attention, aided by the seasonable interference of a good clergyman, has brought about a determination to amend his conduct.[34]

Nineteenth-century artists aimed to inspire respect for figures of authority, as well as for religion itself, where Hogarth could afford to mock them. However, later in the nineteenth century, the more subversive side of Hogarth's art did find imitators. The satirical treatment of the Poor Law Guardians in Cope's painting of 1841 (see below, p.25) looks back to Hogarth; and in the 1850s, the Pre-Raphaelites consciously modelled their paintings of modern life, particularly urban life, on the example set by Hogarth.[35]

In the later eighteenth century, a number of painters produced rustic genre scenes, drawing their inspiration more from Greuze than from Hogarth. Edward Penny, Francis Wheatley, William Redmore Bigg, Thomas Gainsborough and George Morland were all active in this area, and their works, often known through prints, were important precedents for the rustic genre of the early nineteenth century. In the mid-1780s Bigg exhibited several paintings of cottage interiors;[36] in 1793 he showed *Sunday Morning: a Cottage Family going to Church*, now known only from a print (cat.1). This was obviously the inspiration for William Collins' very successful painting of 1837, *Sunday Morning* (cat.8). In each case, the depiction of cottage piety must have been comforting to a middle class audience, fearful of popular revolt. It is signifi-

cant that the theme first appears in British art in 1793, the year of the Terror in France. Other themes which became popular in British art of the late eighteenth century include illustrations of various types of charity, and depictions of self-sufficient peasant families making the most of their limited resources.[37] The peasants depicted by this generation of artists tend to look elegant and well-dressed, partly as a result of the influence of Greuze. Wheatley, especially, was criticised for having copied Greuze to the extent of making his peasants look French rather than English.[38]

Nineteenth-century painters of rural genre, therefore, had many artistic sources to draw on, both from the earlier British tradition and from those of Holland, Flanders and France. Their relationship with these sources was a selective and a creative one, rather than a relationship of slavish dependence. Sources which were the product of very different social circumstances would be modified to fit those of nineteenth-century Britain; often, the borrowings are at the same time an implicit critique of the earlier tradition. The same kind of process continued in the uses made of British genre painting by American artists, as can be seen from a comparison of James Clonney's *Politicians in a Country Bar* (1844; fig.10) with Wilkie's *Village Politicians* (cat.45). For genre painters, earlier art was not simply a source of useful themes and compositions from which to borrow: the modifications made to the tradition could represent a belief in the greater refinement, virtue or intelligence of one age or country over another. Conversely, these echoes of earlier compositions could be used, as in the examples by Faed and Wilkie discussed in this chapter, to draw attention to contemporary social problems.

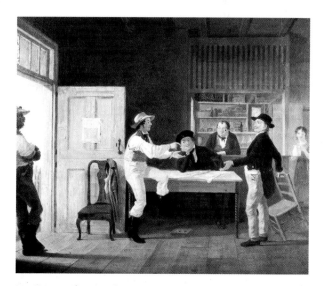

Fig.10 James Clonney, *Politicians in a Country Bar*, 1844. Oil on Canvas, 43.5 x 53.6 cm. New York State Historical Association, Cooperstown.

CHAPTER THREE
Art and Life: The Themes of Rustic Genre Painting in Nineteenth-Century Britain

It is a pleasing sight of a Sunday morning, when the bell is sending its sober melody across the quiet fields, to behold the peasantry in their best finery, with ruddy faces, and modest cheerfulness, thronging tranquilly along the green lanes to church; but it is still more pleasing to see them in the evenings, gathering about the cottage doors, and appearing to exult in the humble comforts and embellishments which their own hands have spread about them.(Washington Irving, *The Sketch Book of Geoffrey Crayon, Gent.*, first published New York, 1819, p.136)

We have looked first at the artistic tradition of genre, since it is now widely recognised by art historians that paintings have as much to do with earlier pictures as with a direct response to nature. However, nineteenth-century rustic genre was also a commentary on the conditions and values of its own time. It needs to be seen, therefore, both in relation to what rural life was actually like, and in relation to middle-class perceptions of rural life. The vast majority of rustic genre paintings conveyed a reassuring, pleasing view of peasant life, similar to the impressions noted by Washington Irving in the above quotation: it is a passage which is paralleled in many paintings and prints, but especially in Bigg's *Sunday Morning* (cat.1), which was originally engraved as one of a pair, the other print showing a happy family outside their cottage, with a spinning wheel, a stack of timber, pigs, a colander of peas, and other products of their labour arranged around them.[39]

In reality life was not easy for the agricultural labourers, tenant farmers and craftsmen who are depicted in these paintings. The day-labourers were the poorest members of British society, a class who suffered from low wages, poor housing and arduous working conditions. Until 1884 they had no political power, no votes (although the working class in the towns got the vote in 1867); they had a reputation for unrest, at least in the first half of the century, when rick-burning and machine-breaking were common features of country life. Most were landless labourers in tied cottages, damp and overcrowded, from which they could be turned out at short notice, living in villages where oppressive social hierarchies were more persistent than in the towns. Their children had limited educational opportunities, and were usually forced by economic necessity to work on the land from an early age. In old age, labourers often ended up in the degrading circumstances of the workhouse, separated from their spouses.

Compared to the urban working class, however, cottagers could seem both fortunate and virtuous: it was widely believed that they were healthier and more beautiful than their urban counterparts, who were stunted by the demands of factory work and the much more intense overcrowding of the rapidly growing towns of the early industrial revolution. Rural unrest was sporadic and much less threatening than the revolutionary potential of the towns. Town workers were seen as irreligious, unpatriotic, readers of seditious newspapers, envious of their employers:[40] the peasantry, by contrast, were regarded as naturally pious, patriotic and virtuous. William Howitt stated this contrast explicitly in 1830:

Overgrown towns and manufactories may have changed, for the worse, the spirit and feelings of their population; in them, 'evil communications may have corrupted good manners'; but in the country at large, there never was a more simple-minded, healthful-hearted and happy race of people than our British peasantry.[41]

By "evil communications", Howitt meant political agitation; by "good manners", probably deference to social superiors, which was so important to the maintenance of the social hierarchy. His description of the characteristics of the peasantry is echoed in many paintings and writings of the nineteenth century. They are represented as "simple-minded", that is, politically unsophisticated and innocent of the temptations of egalitarian ideas; "healthful-hearted", thus innocent also in terms of personal morality; "happy", in other words, contented with their lowly situation in life. Howitt also wrote, in an article on "Cottage Life", published in 1837, of how beautiful the cottages were "in those parts of the country where the violent changes of the time have not been so sensibly felt. Where manufacturers have not introduced their red, staring, bald brick houses, and what is worse, their beershops and demoralization: where, in fact, a more primitive simplicity remains".[42] The "violent changes of the time" - industrialization and, for some, egalitarian ideas -made the perceived survival of "primitive simplicity" in the countryside all the more precious.

It could hardly be denied that the rural labourer was poor; but his health and contentment, it was argued, made such poverty easier to bear. Poverty was regarded as part of the natural order, and as having a positive social function in that it encouraged benevolent feelings on the part of the wealthier members of society.[43] Thus, a certain degree of poverty and even distress was acceptable in paintings because it would stimulate that valuable emotion known as sympathy, humanity or sensibility - the source, according to the philosopher David Hume, of our moral distinctions.[44] As we have seen, Greuze and Diderot would have agreed with him. It is tempting for twentieth-century observers to be cynical about the fashion for sensibility (and there was plenty of cynicism about it at the time), but people really did believe that representations of poverty could encourage the viewers of paintings to become more sympathetic and more generous towards their fellow-men. Aged beggars, widows and rural children were all potential recipients of charity, and their presence in paintings could stimulate similar emotional responses (and the associated pleasurable sensations) to those experienced when giving alms. The language of the critics often employs the discourse of sensibility, as in this comment on Webster's *Good Night!* of 1846 (cat.42):

> We care not what may be the lowliness of the subject, - the strong power of Art, as the evoker of the better feelings of our nature, works ever securely upon the emotions when wielded by the possessor of skill guided by benevolence. Not to be envied is he who looks unmoved on that scene where...'blest contentment' is joined with honest labour, and 'good night' is the harbinger of a well-earned rest.[45]

The man who could look on such a scene unmoved, evidently, was hard-hearted beyond redemption.

The popularity and treatment of particular themes in rustic genre can be linked both to the artistic tradition and to the specific needs of nineteenth-century British society. Some subjects were suggested by earlier paintings; others responded to the contemporary need for paintings that were both didactic and reassuring. Attention was focussed on those areas in which the rural working class displayed virtue, and especially those virtues which were conducive to social order and might be considered to

set a good example to the urban working class. The depiction of happy families in neat cottages, for example, could both reassure the wealthy that the old manners survived in the countryside, and offer an object lesson in parental responsibility and domestic management for the poorer visitors to exhibitions. Cottages had provided inspiration for British novelists, poets, painters and architects since the emergence of the cult of the Picturesque in the late eighteenth century. Landscape painters deliberately sought out the most tumbledown cottages they could find (there are some examples by John Sell Cotman which look as if they are in danger of imminent collapse), but the painters of cottage interiors aimed at creating a sense of well-ordered comfort. Well-swept brick floors and gleaming pans demonstrate the housewife's diligence; pot plants on window sills show the peasant's love of nature; the few possessions often include a large book, presumably the Bible. Paintings of cottage interiors are usually spacious, although contemporary accounts make it clear that most cottages were small and overcrowded, with large families sharing a single bedroom. When, occasionally, artists depicted cramped conditions, as in Arthur Hughes' *Bed Time* (fig.11), the result is shocking to an eye used to more spacious interiors. Many real cottages must also have been extremely dark inside - windows were small - and it is noticeable that many paintings show cottages with open doors, as if acknowledging that this was the only way they would be well lit.

To a twentieth-century eye, the cottage interiors in paintings of the early to mid-nineteenth-century can look absurdly neat and inviting. However, a contemporary observer could well have seen such neatness as a comment, not on rural conditions generally, but on the virtues of the cottager, who was able to make the best of his scant resources. Magdalene Bowles, whose writings offer a close literary parallel to the paintings, contrasted the cottage of the contented, pious and industrious cottager to the hovel of one who lacked these virtues:

> I have often visited two cottages in this village, the inhabitants of which form a striking contrast to each other, and fully prove how much poverty may be softened by regular and active exertions. Both are poor, both with families, receiving the same pay from the parish, in short in <u>every respect</u> upon equal terms in regard to worldly means; but what a difference presents itself when you enter their cottages! One, dark and dismal; the mother in

Fig.11 Arthur Hughes, *Bed Time*, 1862.
Oil on Paper mounted on Canvas, 101.6 x 132 cm. Harris Museum & Art Gallery, Preston.

rags, surrounded by a group of children, whose features are disguised by dirt; the windows broken, and stuffed up with old shreds. The little furniture that you see in this miserable abode is scattered here and there in broken fragments; ...but let us turn to the abode of the other poor family: the hand of industry is there, and mark how cheering are its effects! The house is old, like the other, yet wearing an air of comfort from the cleanliness that surrounds it; the floor is nicely swept: the children employed in assisting their mother - with clean and smiling faces - their clothes not hanging about them in rags, but showing the industry of the parent in the patches which appear upon them; the cups and the saucers, of the meanest sort, no doubt, and some of them broken, are arranged to the best advantage upon the shelf...[a flower in the garden] bespeaks a mind at peace with itself, and contented with the humble lot in which it has pleased GOD to place him.

Magdalene Bowles, the sister of a vicar, was a practical philanthropist who wrote in detail about the benefits to be derived from visiting the poor in their homes and setting up savings clubs for the purchase of blankets, sheets and warm cloth cloaks.[46] Such observers were hardly unaware of the problems faced by poor families in the countryside, but could enjoy looking at pictures which stressed the connection between virtue and comfort.

Cottage interiors are often the setting for scenes of exemplary family life, in which three generations

are shown, from grandparents to small children. The family was an institution of immense importance to nineteenth-century Britain, but it had particular connotations for the working class: a father who was devoted to his children would work hard and avoid the alehouse; his children would grow up to be moral and law-abiding; a careful housewife could overcome the disadvantages of low wages to create a comfortable home. If they were well looked after by their children, old people could enjoy a seat in the chimney corner and avoid having to go to the workhouse. Remaining at home, they could play a valuable role in passing on the rural virtues to their grandchildren, teaching them to pray, read, and in the case of girls, to sew and knit. In comparison to earlier genre painting, the stress on fathers as central elements in the rural home is striking: they openly display their affection for their offspring (and *vice versa*), dandling a baby on their knee or being hugged by the children on their return from work (fig.1; cat.42). There is usually a beautiful woman - mother or eldest daughter - in such paintings: William Howitt, in his article on "Cottage Life" which dates from the same year as Wilkie's *The Cotter's Saturday Night* (cat.49), wrote eloquently of the "sweet faces and lovely forms...seen by the evening passer-by in the light of the ingle, amid the family group, making some smoky-raftered hut a little temple of rare beauty, and filial or sisterly affections."[47]

Rural families are often shown saying grace, listening while the father reads the Bible, or else hearing the children say their prayers before bedtime. There are precedents for these subjects in earlier genre painting (fig.6), but a new emphasis was put on them in nineteenth-century Britain. Godlessness was associated with revolution, and thus the encouragement of religion went hand in hand with efforts to secure the social order. It was noticed that the working class ceased to go to church when they moved to the towns: images of rural piety, therefore, might bring them back to their old habits and protect society against the temptations of radical politics. In an age of intellectual doubt, simple people were regarded as more receptive to the message of the Bible. The well-known preacher, Henry Melvill, argued that this was one of the special blessings intended by God for the poor, which made up for their material disadvantages. While the learned man pores over the Bible in his closet, Melvill said, "the labourer may be sitting down at his cottage door, with his boys and girls drawn around him, explaining to them, from the simply written pages, how great is the Almighty, and how precious is Jesus".[48] Village churches also feature prominently in rural genre paintings. William Collins' *Sunday Morning* (cat.8) was one which occasioned a particularly complacent comment from a reviewer; it was, he wrote, "a composition which cannot be contemplated without feelings of strong emotion, and of self-congratulation in belonging to a country, of the characters and habitual sentiments of so large a proportion of the inhabitants of which it is the unexaggerated representation."[49] It was widely believed that other virtues, such as filial affection (demonstrated in this painting) were the consequence of piety, and thus the depiction of labourers going to church, or singing in a church choir, was doubly reassuring to the middle class.

In scenes of rural family life, children occupy an important role, but they also appear on their own, occasionally working, more often playing or at school. To a twentieth-century eye these children look improbably healthy and apple-cheeked. However, the nineteenth-century perception of a rural childhood was coloured by a consciousness of the appalling conditions in mines and factories. A comment from "a lady" published in William Hone's *Every-Day Book* of 1826 is typical:

> Cottage children are far from being objects of my compassion, for they live in the 'country', which comprehensive word conveys delicious ideas of sun, fresh air, exercise, flowers, shady trees...My pity is reserved for their forlorn little brethren, doomed to breathe the unwholesome atmosphere of crowded manufactures, and close narrow alleys in populous cities![50]

In the paintings of Collins, Webster and Mulready there is a particular emphasis on the happiness of country children, and it is no coincidence that these pictures were painted when the debates over child labour in the mines and factories were at their most intense. Country children also represented hope for the future, and an indication of the moral health of the nation as a whole. Thus, a critic could write in 1836 that the children in Collins' paintings were "those merry-tongued, stout-limbed, honest-hearted urchins, which make us so proud of leading foreigners through our hamlets and homesteads".[51] The language is similar to that of the passage from Howitt, quoted earlier: rustic genre painting encouraged those who wanted to think that urban problems and evidence of disaffection were passing phases, that, at rock bottom, British society was healthy and pure.

Another popular subject was the village school. The development of working class education was closely related to fears of revolution: the supporters of schemes for universal schooling argued that an educated poor would be more likely to respect, rather than to overturn, the social system.[52] J.J.Blunt, the author of *The Duties of a Parish Priest* (1856), considered that schools, preferably under the control of the local clergyman, were vitally important for teaching "habits of punctuality, of honesty, of thrift". He thought that the advance made in the education of the poor over the thirty years from the 1820s to the 1850s had affected "the social system, in the greater patience under privations, and the greater order and self-control under liberty allowed them, exhibited by the labouring classes".[53] Thus, paintings of village schools suggested the virtues of discipline and deference which were seen to be produced by the schools, and showed the children to have only mild vices, such as laziness which makes them late for school, or harmless childish pranks which raise no fears for their underlying moral character. There is a clear differentiation between boys and girls in these paintings: the girls display the caring and submissive traits which will make them good housewives and mothers, while the boys are more energetic and keen to get outside, an indication that the world of farmwork is their true environment, not the world of study. In the paintings, the boys usually outnumber the girls, although contemporary accounts state that boys stayed in school for a shorter time, since they were called away by the demands of field labour.[54]

Charity was an essential element of rural society in the nineteenth century: it was widely recognized that agricultural wages were not sufficient to support a wife and family. Many paintings refer to charity, either directly or indirectly. Some artists showed visitors to the cottage, coming from the big house or the vicarage: these scenes demonstrated harmonious relations between the classes, as well as hinting at the gifts that might be made to offset the inadequacies of agricultural wages (fig.12). Others - and these seem to have been more common - showed the charity of the respectable cottager toward those even less well off, beggars, orphans or the blind (fig.1, cats.16,54). Like other paintings, these illustrated the simple virtues of the rural poor, who were represented as generous despite their own neediness. A late example of this type of painting is Walter Langley's *In Faith and Hope the World may Disagree, but all Mankind's Concern is Charity* (1897; fig.13). This shows a barefoot beggar boy who has been invited into a home and given a bowl of food: the spartan interior implies that the family who live there are poor themselves. The painting was much admired by Leo Tolstoy.[55] The concern that charity would lead to dependence and pauperism was allayed by such paintings, which showed the able-bodied poor as resourceful and self-sufficient, and themselves able to help the orphans, widows or the disabled who were legitimate recipients of charity.

In seventeenth-century art, paintings of peasant merrymakings (the kermesse) were common. However, nineteenth-century British artists carefully avoided the drunkenness and sexual licence that were demonstrated in these earlier paintings. Wilkie's *Village Festival* (1811; Tate Gallery) did show such vices (he meant it as a moral painting and a warning against vice and its consequences) and got a mixed reception. His later *Penny Wedding* (cat.48) received much more approval. In this painting, the fun is kept within acceptable limits: the women are modest, the men are not drunk, and the wealthier members of the community take their place safely amongst their neighbours. The picture gained in credibility by being set in Scotland, and also in the recent past, a place and a time in which it could be believed that members of different classes could mingle freely. A similar subject was the church choir or orchestra, which might also involve villagers of varying social status (cat.2). Such paintings were reassuring because they showed that rural life was not all labour: there were moments of relaxation and time for the finer things in life, such as music. At the same time, they could suggest the survival of harmonious communities in the country-side, although painters liked to create humour by conveying the discomfort of some of the more refined members, as in Webster's *Village Choir* (fig.14) and Hodgson's *Philharmonic Rehearsal in a Farmhouse* (cat.28).

The different customs of the regions were carefully differentiated in genre painting. The Scottish lowlands were used as a model for the rest of the nation in the superiority of their education system (as seen in Wilkie's *Village School*), and also in the apparent existence there of closer relationships between rich and poor. Sir Walter Scott's novels also helped to spread these ideas. The Highlands, on the other hand, were treated like Ireland or remoter parts of Wales: survivals of a wild and primitive way of life, in which greater lawlessness (indicated by whiskey stills or poaching) was compensated for by equally "primitive" virtues, such as those demonstrated in Landseer's genre scenes (cat.29). In portrayals of these areas, artists could depict extreme poverty - tumble-

Fig.12 Carlton Alfred Smith, *A Visit from the Vicarage*, 1886. Oil on Canvas, 73.7 x 94 cm. Christie's Images.

Fig.13 Walter Langley, *In Faith and Hope the World will Disagree, but all Mankind's Concern is Charity*, 1897. Oil on Canvas, 125.7 x 165.7 cm. Courtesy of David Messum Fine Art, London.

down shacks, naked babies, adults ragged and barefoot - without causing offence to their audiences. They could also refer to causes of distress, such as the Highland clearances or to sectarian violence in Ireland, without being seen as subversive. Such paintings might even be seen as a reassuring confirmation of the greater happiness and comfort of the English agricultural labourer. Wilkie's *The Peep'o'Day Boy's Cabin*, which showed a member of an outlawed sect who has returned from a night raid, (fig.15) was exhibited in the same year as Collins' *Sunday Morning*, and a reviewer explicitly compared the two in order to emphasize the virtues of English rural life:

Let the lovers of agitation 'look on this picture and on this' - Mr Collins's 'Sunday Morning', just by; an equally true delineation of an English cottage, of the same class of agricul-tural day-labourers as the inhabitants of the

Fig.14 Thomas Webster, *A Village Choir*, 1847.
Oil on Panel, 60.4 x 91.5 cm. V&A Picture Library.

> Irish cabin...Such as Mr Wilkie has depicted is
> the Irish cabin: such as Mr Collins, with as true
> a pencil, has depicted, is the English
> cottage...Agitation, treason, murder, crowd the
> one; quiet, peace, content, - yea, even in
> poverty, - encompass the other.[56]

By means of a manipulative use of comparison, even a
picture of crime and unrest could be used to reassure
the wealthy and to rebuke agitators who, it is implied,
were also capable of stirring up the English countryside and making it as unhappy as Ireland.

To a twentieth-century observer, many paintings
of nineteenth-century cottage life seem deliberately
mendacious, a denial of the real suffering of the rural
poor. However, there were complex reasons why
artists focussed on the bright side of rural life. Their
public did, indeed, wish to be reassured in a time
when the threat of revolution and disorder was never
far from the surface; but they also had an acute
awareness of the more severe distress of the urban
poor, and a belief that charity, simple faith and the
domestic virtues could alleviate social problems.
Paintings of happy, healthy rural children might
remind viewers of the iniquities of child labour in the

Fig.15 Sir David Wilkie, *The Peep'o' Day Boy's Cabin in the West of Ireland*,
1835-6. Oil on Canvas, 125.7 x 175.3 cm. © Tate Gallery, London 1998.

mines and factories; depictions of cottagers practising
the virtues of thrift, filial affection and piety could be
seen as demonstrations of potential solutions to
worrying problems in both town and country. Even the
most apparently comforting paintings, therefore, could
appeal to a sensitivity towards such problems, rather
than a hard-hearted indifference towards them.
Alongside these comforting paintings, there were
others which raised social issues explicitly, sometimes
in a controversial and challenging way, and these will
be the subject of the next chapter.

CHAPTER FOUR
Philanthropy and Politics: Rural Genre Paintings and Reform

By her vivid representations of rags and roofless cabins - of the daring violators of custom-house regulations - of the victims of the game laws - of criminals, the offspring of legal injustice - by her bold satires of the foolish eccentricities of men armed with power, or endowed with wealth, she (Painting) has become a great teacher on the side of Nature, and the auxiliary of honest labour. (Anon., "The Place of the Fine Arts in the Natural System of Society", *Douglas Jerrold's Shilling Magazine*, 31 July 1847)

As we have seen from the preceding section, the majority of rural genre paintings were reassuring to their upper and middle-class viewers, assuaging fears of unrest and emphasizing the survival of rural virtue and contentment. To a large extent, they encouraged complacency and nostalgia. There were some paintings, however, which deliberately focussed on topical and controversial issues. These attracted widespread attention, even notoriety, in their day. Following the precedent set by Hogarth, painters highlighted abuses of power and stirred the consciences of the ruling classes, thus contributing to debates which were, ultimately, to lead to reforms which would improve the condition of the rural labourer, and that of the working class in general.

In the second half of the eighteenth century, the poetry of Thomas Gray, Robert Burns and William Wordsworth encouraged their readers to feel sympathy for the poor, and to accept that the poor were as capable as the rich of depths of feeling. Wordsworth even claimed, in his Preface to *Lyrical Ballads* (1800), that rustic life was the best place to observe the basic passions of men:

> Low and rustic life was generally chosen because in that situation the essential passions of the heart find a better soil in which they can attain their maturity, are less under restraint, and speak a plainer and more emphatic language...being less under the action of social vanity they [rustics] convey their feelings and notions in simple and unelaborated expressions.[57]

Wordsworth, like many other English writers of the eighteenth century, was influenced by the ideas of Jean-Jacques Rousseau, who argued that man was naturally good but was corrupted by society. The peasant, therefore, being closer to nature, was morally and physically healthier than those who lived in cities or in mansions. Rousseau's ideas were especially influential in English educational theory, but they were also pervasive in many of the novels and poems of the eighteenth century.[58]

There is a direct link between such ideas in poetry and their expression in a painting like Wilkie's *Blind Fiddler* (fig.1). In this picture, the poor are shown not only as charitable, but also as possessing sensitivity towards music. Critics recognised that Wilkie was going well beyond the stereotypical comedy of rustic character in attempting complex mixtures of emotion, as in "the contest of feelings on the face of the eldest girl, desirous as she seems of frowning her roguish brother into decorum, and yet compelled to laugh by the absurdity of his gestures." This quotation comes from a review in the *Morning Post*, a conservative paper, which ends with the declaration that the painting "cannot fail to interest every mind not so desperately fastidious, as to refuse to enter into the feelings of the inferior classes of society" and a verse from Gray's *Elegy*:

> Let not ambition mock their useful toil,
> Their homely joys and destiny obscure,
> Nor grandeur hear with a disdainful smile,
> The short and simple annals of the poor.[59]

Many rustic genre paintings deal with these "homely joys", the appreciation of which was seen as an antidote to aristocratic disdain for the feelings of the poor.

Another reviewer, Robert Hunt (a friend of Wilkie) writes in terms very similar to those of Wordsworth's Preface when he says that Wilkie and his rival, Edward Bird "paint the human passions as they are the spontaneous effusions of the heart in humble and domestic life, and of strong, natural feeling, unchecked by any artificial refinements of polished society."[60] Wilkie chose subjects which can be directly linked to poems by Wordsworth, Gray and Burns (although he resisted suggestions that Wordsworth should supply him with subjects).[61] Burns, and Wordsworth in his early life, had radical political sympathies: the claim that the poor were capable of noble feelings was potentially subversive. Sir Walter Scott noted in 1824 that the "affectation of attributing noble and virtuous sentiments, to the persons least qualified by habit or education to entertain them" [i.e. the working classes] was "the groundwork of a sort of intellectual jacobinism".[62] Scott, Beaumont, and probably Wilkie, were able to reconcile the new emphasis on the deeper feelings of the poor with political conservatism - and readers of Burns were able to ignore his radicalism - but there remained a new seriousness in rustic genre, which challenged older justifications of the social hierarchy.

An early painting by William Mulready, *The Carpenter's Shop* (untraced), exemplifies this new approach.[63] Exhibited in 1809, it draws some elements from Wilkie's *Blind Fiddler*, but concentrates on the serious rather than the humorous aspects of the life of the artisan. In a setting which emphasizes the hard labour of the carpenter's life, he pauses to look lovingly at his wife and baby, with as much tenderness of feeling as would be depicted at any higher social level. Richard and Samuel Redgrave gave a very full description of this painting in their *Century of Painters of the English School* (1866): their account carries some weight since Richard, as well as being a genre painter himself (see cat.37) was a personal friend of Mulready's. To them, the picture was clearly meant to inform the rich about the realities of life amongst the poor, in a way that was truthful and unexaggerated: "It has been tritely said that one half of the world does not know how the other half lives; here, at least, the upper ten thousand may look upon the every-day life of the lower ten million under, perhaps, its best aspect."[64] The painting was highly praised by contemporary critics, but failed to win the prize for "Familiar Life" which had been announced by the British Institution in that year. The prize went instead to Sharp's *Music Master*, a comic genre painting, and Mulready was criticized for asking too much, 300 guineas, for a painting which had "more of the elaborate finish of manual labour than of genius".[65] *The Carpenter's Shop* remained unsold until 1812, when it was bought by Lady Swinburne, wife of Sir John Swinburne, a radical and patron of Mulready. There are strong hints of radicalism in Mulready's own views, and Kathryn Heleniak, in her study of his life and work, describes him as a professed democrat who kept a low profile, but whose "devotion to everyday scenes can perhaps be linked to his underlying faith in the common man."[66] On this occasion, the Directors of the British Institution seem to have retreated in the direction of a politically safer view of rustic life than the one offered by Mulready - as was to happen again in the more

famous case of Wilkie's *Distraining for Rent* (1815).

Debates over the capacity of the lower classes for feeling were inextricably linked to debates over Parliamentary reform and education. The central issue was this: was the rustic a comic idiot, or was he a man like any other, responsive to education and capable of exercising a share of political power? Wilkie's celebrated painting, *The Village Politicians* (cat.45), at first sight might seem to support the traditional view, showing characters who were too ludicrous to offer any real threat to the social hierarchy. In addition to referring to Teniers, it draws on a long tradition of ridiculing the pretensions of artisans to participation in politics, in popular prints and, from the 1790s, counter-revolutionary tracts such as Hannah More's *Village Politics* (1793).[67] However, Wilkie avoids the crude stereotypes of these earlier precedents, making his debaters look more human and, in some cases, markedly more intelligent. It was this quality which presumably caused Fuseli to label the work "dangerous"; it enabled later commentators, and American artists, to regard the painting as an image suitable for a developing democracy.[68] Wilkie's own attitude to Parliamentary reform is hard to fathom - it is clear that he did not want his conservative patrons, such as Lord Mulgrave, to think he was pro-reform - but he was a close friend of Benjamin Robert Haydon, who supported reform, and there is evidence that he took an interest in the movement.[69] Later on, Mulready, less cautious than Wilkie in revealing his political colours, produced a painting which was unambiguously pro-reform, in his *Returning from the Hustings*, a clear criticism of the corruption of the old system at the time of the agitation over the Reform Bill in the early 1830s.[70]

During the course of the nineteenth century, successive Reform Acts widened the franchise until, in 1867, the town artisan, and in 1884 the rural labourer, became voters. In this same period literacy was increasing, partly as a result of state efforts to reform the education of the poor. In 1815, Mulready exhibited a painting of a schoolroom, *Idle Boys*, which was bought by a politician, Earl Grey, Whig M.P. and later Prime Minister, whose party set up select committees to discuss education between 1816 and 1818, and whose ministry took up their recommendations 13 years later. A year earlier Wilkie had begun his *Village School* (fig.4), which appears to show the Bell and Lancaster system of using child monitors to teach large numbers of children. Mulready's later schoolroom painting, *The Last In* (cat.31), looks very old-fashioned and far from topical, but in fact it was painted at a time of educational reforms: in 1833 Grey's government made the first grant of £20,000 to aid in the construction of schoolhouses, Select Committees met in 1834 and 1835 to investigate the means of establishing a system of national education, and the first grant was made towards the training of teachers in 1835.[71] Mulready's primitive, overcrowded interior, with its sadistic schoolmaster, shows the old type of village school, soon to be superseded by the new National Schools and, as Mulready depicts it, badly in need of reform. Educational reforms continued throughout the nineteenth century, with the Education Act of 1870 laying the basis for the modern system.

Another area of controversy lay in relations between rich and poor: in the countryside, this meant relations between landlords and their tenant farmers or labourers. Wilkie seems consciously to have chosen to approach this theme in a challenging way. In *Distraining for Rent* (cat.47) he depicts a farmer and his family, being deprived of their goods by unsympathetic bailiffs. The pathos is unrelieved by comedy: indeed, Wilkie declared that he had painted the picture because he did not want to be known only as a comic painter.[72] The farmer and his family are tragic, the bailiff and his men sinister and unsympathetic, the neighbours outraged and supportive. Haydon and Abraham Raimbach (who engraved many of Wilkie's paintings and was his close associate and business partner) tell us that it was considered to be a "factious" attack on landlords - that is, on the aristocrats who were Wilkie's patrons and the ruling spirits of both the Royal Academy and the British Institution. Sir George Beaumont complained that Wilkie had not made it clear why the farmer was having his goods distrained: "he might have shown that he was a dissipated tenant" - in other words, he might have shown that the landowner was not to blame.[73] A reviewer in a conservative paper, *Bell's Weekly Messenger*, was clearly discomfited by the absence of a reassuring moral:

> The subject is ill chosen; there are a thousand incidents in domestic life which a painter, of imagination and talents like Mr Wilkie, could have selected, with a view of expressing the various passions of human nature, and at the same time conveying to the spectator's mind some pleasing humour or instructive moral...but there is an attempt to pourtray (sic) nothing but despair, cruelty, and oppression, in the prosecution of a legal right. The conception is torturing to sensibility...[74]

It was "torturing to sensibility", presumably, because sensibility involved sympathy and benevolence towards the poor and unfortunate, but was not meant to stir up indignation against social injustice.

The later history of *Distraining for Rent* confirms that it was seen as dangerous: the Directors of the British Institution bought it, but did not put it on show, and were happy to sell it to Abraham Raimbach, who wanted to buy it so that he could make an engraving from it.[75] A similar fate befell C.W.Cope's picture, *The Board of Guardians - the Widow's Application for Bread* (1841: fig.16). This was a highly topical painting, a criticism of the New Poor Law of 1834, which aimed to end outdoor relief for paupers by granting them help only if they entered the workhouse. A whole spectrum of responses by the members of the board is shown - some listen sympathetically, or reach into a purse, but others are hard-hearted or indifferent. Cope claimed that it was referred to in a report in *The Times* on the debates on the Poor Law, but no-one bought it, and Cope, as a result, abandoned such socially conscious themes.[76] Such paintings were analogous to the novels of Charles Dickens and other writers in drawing attention to the shortcomings of certain members of the upper and middle classes. However, in painting, unlike literature, the effect was immediate, and accessible to the illiterate. Artists who wished to make social comments faced a twofold problem: the painting might be seen as destructive to public morality, and therefore not suitable for exhibition; and they might fail to find a wealthy collector willing to purchase the painting. They were thus encouraged to aim at "pleasing humour" and an "instructive moral" rather than hard-hitting social criticism.

If pictures like these challenged the belief in the social harmony of the countryside, pictures of poaching cast doubt on the virtues of the farm

Fig.16 Charles West Cope, *The Board of Guardians-the Widow's Application for Bread*, 1841. Oil on Canvas, 58.4 x 91.4 cm. Christie's Images.

labourer. Poaching was a chronic problem in ninteenth-century rural England, and one which, according to conservative views, led to other crimes: the poacher was likely to neglect his family, drink in the alehouse, and graduate to rioting and rick-burning. As the Marquis of Lansdowne said in a debate in Parliament in May 1828, "there could be no doubt that poaching was the initiation for other crime - that it accustomed the lower orders of the people to midnight adventures, and to habits the most remote from regular, and wholesome industry."[77] The poacher was thus the antithesis of the hard-working, church-going labourer who is depicted surrounded by his loving family in so many rural genre paintings. Painters could use the poacher as a substitute for Hogarth's idle apprentice, in a series of pictures which would demonstrate the ill effects of this species of rural crime. This is what Edward Bird did in his series of six paintings in 1813: the surviving painting shows the poacher in prison, listening to a clergyman who reads from the Bible (fig.9). Bird's own political views were conservative, and his paintings had messages which were thoroughly in accordance with conservative thinking.[78] Most paintings of poachers, however, were more ambiguous, and probably had the effect of drawing attention to laws which many saw as unfair, or to the poverty which made poaching necessary for survival, rather than to the moral preached by Bird. The paintings of poachers by Thomas Wade and James Campbell (cats.40,4) could certainly be read in this way. Poaching was also a cause of fights, even of fatalities, in the countryside, an issue to which Mulready's *Interior of an English Cottage*, originally called *The Gamekeeper's Cottage* (fig.17) draws attention. The painting was exhibited as the Night Poaching Bill was being debated in the Commons, and was thus very topical: the wife has waited up until late at night for her husband, the gamekeeper, who may have been risking his life in a battle with poachers.[79]

Paintings of emigration themes were also popular, and, like poaching scenes, they referred to a social issue which was far from comforting. Emigration was seen by many, on all sides of the political spectrum, as a solution to the problems of rural England. Popular magazines, in the 1850s especially, carried stories about the prosperous life that could be led in the colonies, where there was enough land for everyone. However, artists often focussed on the human cost of emigration - the sadness of leaving loved ones behind, of bidding farewell to places and communities without any prospect of return (fig.18). Thomas Faed's *Sunday in the Backwoods* (cat.17) showed the old virtues carried over to the colonies (a popular theme in

Fig.17 William Mulready, *The Interior of an English Cottage*, 1828. Oil on Panel, 62.2 x 50.5 cm. The Royal Collection. © 1998 Her Majesty The Queen.

optimistic views of emigration) but his view of the emigrants' life is a bleak one. In another painting, *The Last of the Clan* (fig.19), he refers explicitly to the Highland Clearances which had made the exodus necessary. In the eighteenth century, Oliver Goldsmith's references to emigration in his poems, *The Traveller* and *The Deserted Village*, had similarly viewed emigration as a sad necessity brought about by the greed of the rich. Richard Redgrave quoted lines from the former in the catalogue when he exhibited *The Emigrant's Last Sight of Home* (cat.37). He was reproved for his choice of verse by a critic who declared: "The time is gone by for such maudlin stuff as this, and artists, if they would minister to the requirements of the age in 'Britain's peopled shore', and in new homes 'beyond the western main' would do wisely to adopt a more ennobling view of a great social and political movement."[80] Once again, the artist was encouraged to convey an "instructive moral" rather than to raise questions which might cause disquiet amongst the middle classes.

There are other paintings which have a more indirect relationship with the social issues which concerned nineteenth-century reformers. Cottage interiors, for example, sometimes seem to focus deliberately on areas which were highlighted in campaigns for better working class housing. Webster's *Good Night!* (cat.42) has a very prominent bowl of extremely clean water in the foreground, at a time when the role of the water supply in carrying cholera was beginning to be recognised. It also shows a cottage that is full of fresh air from an open window - when alternative theories of infection put much emphasis on the circulation of air. By contrast, Arthur Hughes' *Bed Time* (fig.11) appears to show the kind of overcrowded cottage that worried reformers who feared that inadequate bedrooms led to incest and other forms of sexual immorality. One prominent reformer, Angela Burdett-Coutts, bought several rustic genre paintings, including Faed's *Home and the Homeless* (cat.16) and Collinson's *The Writing Lesson* (cat.10), so that in this case, at least, we can say that rustic genre was compatible with reformist views, rather than denying the necessity of change or acting as a soothing substitute for action.[81]

In the end, it is very difficult to assess how far paintings contributed to improvements in the condition of the rural labourer in nineteenth-century Britain, but these examples do at least show that they were not solely a celebration of the status quo. Like much of the literature of the time, they both challenge and confirm prejudices, both raise social issues and soothe the anxieties caused by them, and they sometimes do this within a single painting. Artists highlighted issues that were topical, encouraging their audience to think about areas of national life that suggested the need for reforms: the Poor Law, emigration, poaching, the education of the poor. Even the cosy cottage interiors, which might seem to us to be purely reassuring, had a radical aspect in their promotion of a belief in the emotional capacities of the working class.

Fig.19 Thomas Faed, *The Last of the Clan*, 1865. Oil on Canvas, 144.8 x 182.9 cm. Glasgow Museums: Art Gallery & Museum, Kelvingrove.

Fig.18 James Collinson, *Answering the Emigrant's Letter*, 1850. Oil on Panel, 70.1 x 91.2 cm. © Manchester City Art Galleries.

CHAPTER FIVE
"Circulation among all Classes of the Community": Patrons, Exhibitions and Prints

...private patronage...[calls] alike on art to decorate the dwelling of the noble, and embellish the abode of the peasant - to pour a ray or two of its light on the thick darkness of sullen ignorance, and mingle its fuller and brighter beam with the sunshine of learning and taste. (Sir David Wilkie, quoted in A.Cunningham, Life of Wilkie, 1843, III, p.147)

A repeated theme of the nineteenth-century critical literature on rural genre painting is that it appeals to everyone, whatever their rank in life, because it touches on emotions common to all. From a twentieth-century perspective, we can see how different classes might view these paintings in different ways: the wealthy spectator would be stimulated to feelings of paternalistic benevolence, the poorer viewer would empathize with the characters or regard them as an object lesson for his or her own life. The nature of the engagement different classes had with the paintings varied, too: only the wealthy would be able to afford to buy one of these paintings and study it over time. The poor would have to make do with the shorter acquaintance afforded by public exhibitions, or with the various translations of the painting into prints.

At the beginning of the nineteenth century, the main buyers of rustic genre painting came from the landed aristocracy. Wilkie had a whole circle of titled patrons, from the Prince Regent downwards: the most faithful being Lord Mulgrave, Sir George Beaumont, and Sir Robert Peel; other buyers of his genre paintings included Lord Mansfield (who bought *The Village Politicians*, cat.45) and the Duke of Gloucester. It is noteworthy that many of his patrons were actively involved in politics, mainly in a conservative capacity, although one exception to this was Samuel Whitbread II, a well-known Radical who bought *The Cut Finger* (cat.46). It is likely, therefore, that Wilkie's buyers would have been very much alive to the topical references in his work, and to the controversial political issues on which it touched. These titled patrons generally owned Old Masters as well as modern British paintings, and regarded themselves as connoisseurs who could compare the technique of Wilkie with that of, for example, Teniers or Steen. Haydon, who deplored the taste for "Dutch" minuteness in art, wrote of having seen "C-, M-, D-, L-, and all the ministers of England, squeeze to a small P- of W- of a servant washing a child's face with her hand, while one eye being only seen is squeezed up in agony" (probably Canning, Mulgrave, Dundas and Liverpool).[82] The Prince Regent, later George IV, bought Wilkie's *Penny Wedding*, and also Bird's *Country Choristers* (cats.48,2): both paintings offer a reassuring vision of a well-behaved populace, with the classes co-existing in harmony with one another, particularly suitable for the royal collection. Collins' *Rustic Civility* (cat.7), with its overtones of feudal "obeisance" was also, appropriately, bought by an aristocrat, the Duke of Devonshire. The buyers of Mulready's rustic genre paintings also included politicians, Earl Grey and Sir John Swinburne; the latter, who was a Radical, was a particularly faithful patron.[83]

By the 1830s and 1840s, the patronage of the landed aristocracy was giving way, in genre painting as in British art generally, to that of the new collectors: men of lower or middle-class origin who had made (or inherited) money from industry or commerce, and who were keen to invest in contemporary painting rather than in old masters which might turn out to be forgeries. One of the most prominent of these was John Sheepshanks, who bought a total of 30 paintings by Mulready, 11 of these direct from the artist, as well as rural genre paintings by Wilkie, Webster, Collins, Landseer, and Hardy.[84] Sheepshanks was a philanthropist, who donated his collection to the South Kensington Museum (now the Victoria and Albert Museum) in the hope that it would be seen by large numbers of people. He specifically asked that it should be open to the public on Sundays after divine service, a time when working people would be able to see it. The museum's curator, Richard Redgrave (who was, of course, a genre painter himself) spoke eloquently of the benefits this would bring to the working class of the city. In a lecture given in 1857, Redgrave said: "The great feature of the new museum is, no doubt, the arrangement made for lighting and opening it to the operative class after their working hours. Half the vices of the labouring man arise from the closeness, dirt, and discomforts of his home. In order to avoid this, he leaves his family for the beershop or taproom..." but the new gallery would provide the means "even if only for a few hours, of keeping thousands, and tens of thousands, from the haunts of vice and debauchery...of enjoying themselves lawfully, with wives and little ones..."[85] Such an audience sounds like the figures depicted in many genre paintings, family groups engaged in morally healthy activities, away from the temptations of the alehouse.

Another middle-class collector who had a taste for rustic genre painting was Sidney Cartwright, whose pictures became the nucleus of the important collection at Wolverhampton Art Gallery: amongst the pictures he bought were Faed's *Sunday in the Backwoods*, Hardy's *Preparing for Dinner* and *The Dismayed Artist*,   and Hodgson's *Philharmonic Rehearsal* (cats.17,22,24,28). He owned a factory which produced children's toys, and seems to have been a relatively enlightened employer: he told a government commission in 1841 that he believed the moral character of the poor was damaged by their extreme poverty, and he advocated the education of children up to the age of nine; on the other hand, like many other factory owners, he employed older children in his factory.[86] He and his wife, who were childless, had in their collection many pictures which featured carefree rural children: his wife left them to the local art gallery in 1887, declaring that she was carrying out her husband's wish that they "should be dedicated to some public purpose in a manner calculated to impart general pleasure".[87] It is tempting to speculate that, by buying paintings of rural children and making them available to the poor, the couple felt that they were compensating, both for their own childlessness and for their exploitation of child labour in their factory. Two other paintings in the exhibition which were bought by city tradesmen were Mulready's *The Last In* and Collins' *Sunday Morning* (cats.31,8). The Mulready was bought by Robert Vernon, who made a collection of modern British paintings and presented it to the National Gallery in 1847; it included other rustic genre paintings by Mulready, Webster and Wilkie. Vernon, like Sheepshanks, evidently felt that rustic genre was an important area of British expertise in contemporary painting.[88] Collins' *Sunday Morning* was bought by George Knott, a city grocer.[89]

Redgrave and Sheepshanks were not alone in regarding art as a vehicle for social and moral improvement in the working class. In 1839, Samuel Carter Hall had founded the monthly *Art Union* in an attempt to bring art to a wider public, arguing that "a collection of pictures powerfully helps to thin our poorhouses and prisons...men to whom public galleries are open will seldom be found in public-houses."[90] As Richard Redgrave's lecture suggests, the public for art was widening in the mid-nineteenth century. The figures for museum and exhibition attendance in this period are staggeringly high, and from contemporary accounts it is clear that much of the audience for art was working class.[91] The large crowds raised fears for the safety of the pictures in the Sheepshanks Gallery at the South Kensington Museum.[92] In 1857 strenuous efforts were made to encourage the working classes to visit the Art Treasures exhibition in Manchester: special trains were laid on and excursions of factory workers organised by employers. The most spectacular of these must have been the visit by 2,500 workers from Titus Salt's Saltaire: they arrived in their Sunday best, complete with two bands. The chairman of the organisers, Thomas Fairbairn, claimed that 600,000 to 700,000 working people had seen the exhibition.[93]

It was widely believed that art would have a morally beneficial effect on these large crowds, partly because art exhibitions provided an alternative to the public house, but also because pictures could teach moral lessons. Rustic genre had a particular role to play in this, depicting rural families who made the best of limited resources as an object lesson for the city masses, and demonstrating the link between the virtues of piety, family affection, frugality and happiness. In a lengthy review of the Art Treasures exhibition in October 1857, Robert Lamb wrote:

> And not simply may subjects strictly religious exert a moral influence; the painter who represents a virtuous and ennobling deed of any kind, is a benefactor of his species...Is there not a lesson in the child praying on its mother's knee, in the hearty, rollicking face of the schoolboy, in the happy country scene, in the way-side flowers, in the running brook, in the golden sunset, in the cottager's home, in the old churchyard? There is not a sunny spot or a dark shadow on the face of nature which is not calculated to improve the heart, if the eye that looks on it be pure and simple.[94]

Such subjects would have a particular resonance for exhibition visitors who had been brought up in the country, as so many of the urban working class had at this period: they were a reminder, then, of simple childhood virtues and a counterweight to the corruption and temptations of city life.

Attempts were made, also, to extend the patronage of art down the social scale. In 1837, in emulation of similar organisations in Germany, the Art Union of London was set up. For an annual fee of one guinea, the subscriber got an engraving of a famous painting and the chance to enter a lottery and win a painting from one of the current year's exhibitions. Thus, people of relatively modest incomes could consider themselves as, at least, potential patrons of art. By 1844, the subscription stood at almost 15,000, and the Art Union was buying hundreds of paintings each year.[95] The committee of the Art Union, and its supporters in Parliament, were keen to establish free museums and exhibitions in order to make art accessible to the working class. They held annual exhibitions of the works chosen as prizes; from 1842 onwards, these were open free to the general public.[96] Prizewinners were allowed to select the paintings themselves, and there were repeated complaints that their poor taste was lowering the standard of British art. In 1843 W.M.Thackeray defended the Art Unions against the criticism of the *Athenaeum*, who said that they would lead to the degradation of art, by declaring that "the poet and artist is called upon to appeal to the few no longer. His profit and fame are with the many...If you have something that is worth the telling - something for the good of mankind - it is better to take it to a hundred tinkers or tailors than to one duke or two dandies (speaking with perfect respect of both)".[97] Of the paintings chosen as prizes, the vast majority were landscapes, but between 18 and 28% were genre scenes. One of these was Hughes' *Bed Time* (fig.11), chosen by an Art Union winner in 1862.[98]

Another way in which these images reached a wider public was through prints. In the late eighteenth century, rustic genre became popular for decorative prints - often produced in pairs - by artists such as Francis Wheatley and William Redmore Bigg. Wilkie followed Hogarth's example in having his works engraved, mainly as a means of increasing his income. He was fastidious in his choice of engravers, and Abraham Raimbach, who eventually became his preferred engraver, produced very fine, extremely meticulous engravings, which successfully conveyed much of the characterisation and expression for which Wilkie was renowned (fig.20). Both Wilkie and Raimbach believed strongly in the dissemination of art amongst the lower classes of society.[99] Through the sending of prints abroad, Wilkie's work became well known in France, Germany and the United States.[100] Other rustic genre painters, including Mulready, Collins, Faed and Webster, also had their work engraved. The best of these prints could convey not only character but also some sense of the subtle lighting effects achieved in cottage interiors: the work of Lumb Stocks is particularly successful in this respect (cats.19,44). Such fine prints were not cheap - the print of *The Village Politicians*, for example, sold for 2 guineas in 1812[101] - but they were much cheaper than an oil painting, which would sell for several hundred pounds. Their probable destination, therefore, would have been middle-class homes rather than those of artisans or labourers.

Fine prints were themselves translated into cheaper prints, either through pirated engravings, or through reproductions in newspapers, or in specially produced books of prints such as *The Wilkie Gallery* of 1851. *The Village Politicians* and *Distraining for Rent*, for example, were both issued as part of a series of

"Cartoons for the People" with the *London Journal* in 1848 and 1849 (copies of these are held in the Print Room of the British Museum). Marcia Pointon has shown how, in France, a range of prints, many of very poor quality, were derived from Wilkie's *Blind Man's Buff* in the early nineteenth century, by being copied either from Raimbach's engraving or from each other;[102] the British Museum holds a similar range of prints - both French and British - after *The Blind Fiddler*, including an embossed tableau intended for the blind. The extreme examples of such derivations can be very crude, and preserve little of the original beyond the interest of the story. The faces of the characters, especially, betray the differing levels of skill of the painter, the fine engraver and the hack engraver, although the latter sometimes tried to improve on the original by, for example, making the blind fiddler's wife more beautiful. The reputations of rustic genre painters may have suffered more than most from this translation into cheaper forms, because their subject matter was regarded as particularly suitable for an unlettered audience.

It is, therefore, true that rustic genre painting was circulated amongst all classes of the community (as the quotation at the head of Chapter 2 suggests) - but in very different forms according to the social level at which it was seen. The qualities of colour and brushwork appreciated by the connoisseurs who bought the paintings were largely lost in the translation into graphic media, and in their cheaper forms the skills of the artists in drawing, composition and characterization would have been hard to discern. However, where the engravings were made directly from the original paintings the resulting prints could be of very fine quality. The growth of the public for art, and the dissemination of art through prints, exhibitions and the Art Unions, meant that rustic genre reached a wide market, at a time when many influential observers firmly believed in the power of art to influence the moral behaviour of the masses.

Fig.20 Abraham Raimbach *after* Sir David Wilkie *Distraining For Rent*, 1828. Engraving, 41.2 x 61.6 cm. Yale Center for British Art, Paul Mellon Collection.

Cat.2 *Country Choristers* (1810), EDWARD BIRD

Cat.6 *The Legend* (1864-78), GEORGE PAUL CHALMERS

Cat.8 *Sunday Morning* (1836), WILLIAM COLLINS

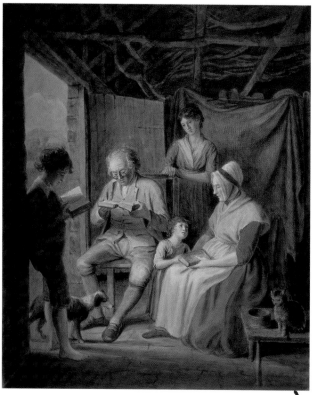

Cat.5 *Sunday Morning - "La Lecture de la Bible"* (c.1812),
ALEXANDER CARSE

Cat.4 *The Wife's Remonstrance* (1858), JAMES CAMPBELL

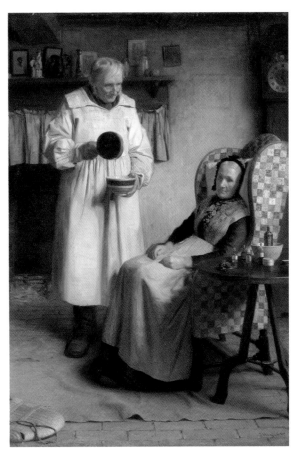

Cat.26 *The Invalid* (c.1889), JAMES HAYLLAR

Cat.21 *The Poachers Alarmed* (1844), ALFRED DOWNING FRIPP

Cat.7 *Rustic Civility* (1832), WILLIAM COLLINS

Cat.15 *The Visit of the Patron and Patroness to the Village School* (1851), THOMAS FAED

Cat.10 *The Writing Lesson* (1855), JAMES COLLINSON

Cat.25 *A Schule Skailin'* (1846), SIR GEORGE HARVEY

Cat.11 *Cottage Interior at Rievaulx, Yorkshire* (1840), CHARLES WEST COPE

Cat.12 *Cottage Interior* (c.1840), CHARLES WEST COPE

Cat.16 *Home and the Homeless* (1856), THOMAS FAED

Cat.17 *Sunday in the Backwoods* (1859-63), THOMAS FAED

Cat.20 *School is Out* (1889), ELIZABETH ADELA ARMSTRONG FORBES

Cat.31 *The Last In* (1835), WILLIAM MULREADY

Cat.22 *Preparing for Dinner* (1854), FREDERICK DANIEL HARDY

Cat.23 *Expectation: Interior of a Cottage with a Mother and Children* (1854), FREDERICK DANIEL HARDY

Cat.24 *The Dismayed Artist* (1866), FREDERICK DANIEL HARDY

Cat.28 *A Philharmonic Rehearsal in a Farmhouse* (1860), JOHN EVAN HODGSON

Cat.27 *A Fisherman's Cottage* (1810), THOMAS HEAPHY

Cat.29 *Interior of a Highlander's House* (c.1831), SIR EDWIN LANDSEER

Cat.37 *The Emigrant's Last Sight of Home* (1859), RICHARD REDGRAVE

Cat.41 *A Stitch in Time* (c.1868), THOMAS WADE

Cat.40 *The Poacher's Home* (c.1868), THOMAS WADE

Cat.42 *Good Night!* (1846), THOMAS WEBSTER

Cat.43 *A Tea Party* (1862), THOMAS WEBSTER

Cat.45 *The Village Politicians* (1805), SIR DAVID WILKIE

Cat.46 *The Cut Finger* (1809), SIR DAVID WILKIE

Cat.47 *Distraining for Rent* (1815), SIR DAVID WILKIE

Cat.49 *The Cotter's Saturday Night* (1832-7), SIR DAVID WILKIE

Cat.48 *The Penny Wedding* (1818), SIR DAVID WILKIE

Cat.52 *Sketch for The Penny Wedding* (1817), SIR DAVID WILKIE

CATALOGUE OF EXHIBITS

Note: the catalogue is arranged by names of artists in alphabetical order. Prints are given under the name of the artist of the painting from which the print was derived. Where there are several works by one artist, paintings are given first, then drawings and prints.

1. Sunday Morning: a Cottage Family Going to Church (1795)

WILLIAM NUTTER (1754-1802) after
WILLIAM REDMORE BIGG (1755-1828)
Stipple etching
50 x 58 cm.
Provenance: Purchased from Messrs Evans, 1860.
The British Museum

William Redmore Bigg produced a large number of paintings of cottage genre in the late eighteenth and early nineteenth centuries, many of which are now known only from titles in exhibition catalogues or from prints. This print is based on a painting shown at the Royal Academy in 1793 (no.58). As far as we can tell, his work emphasized the happiness of the cottager and the benevolence of the gentry: amongst the surviving paintings are *A Lady and Children Relieving a Distressed Cottager* (1781, Philadelphia Museum of Art) and a pair in the Yale Center for British Art, *The Benevolent Heir Restoring an Old Cottager, Confined for Debt, to his Family* and *The Severe Steward; or Unfortunate Tenant* (1797, 1801).[1] His cottage family in *Sunday Morning* is extremely well-dressed and refined in features. They provide an exemplary demonstration of family virtues: the mother tenderly ties a scarf around the grandfather's balding head, while the baby sits in front of him, her hand on his, and the little girl uses a stick to chase the dog away from the old man's sore leg. Meanwhile, the eldest daughter waits patiently at the gate, turning solicitously towards her family. The presence of no less than three books (a Bible and two prayerbooks), and the obvious effort required to get the grandfather to church, both stress the importance of religion to this rural family.

It seems likely that Bigg's cottage scenes exercised a wide influence, not only in Britain but also further afield. William Collins' later painting of a similar subject (cat.8) adapts Bigg's composition but

1

gives it a more plebeian tone. Across the Atlantic, the interiors of the Oak Hill Mansion from Salem, Massachusetts (1800-01) which are now housed in the Museum of Fine Arts, Boston, contain two copies, presumably based on prints after Bigg, attributed to Michele Felice Corno, an Italian immigrant artist.[2]

1. There is a comprehensive catalogue entry on the first of these in Richard Dorment, *British Painting in the Philadelphia Museum of Art from the Seventeenth through the Nineteenth Century*, Philadelphia Museum of Art in association with Weidenfeld and Nicolson, London, 1986, pp.24-27. The titles for all three paintings are those given in the Royal Academy catalogues for 1781, 1797 and 1801 respectively.
2. The copy of *Sunday Morning* is over the fireplace in the parlour, while a copy of its companion, *Saturday Evening*, is over the fireplace in the dining room.

2. Country Choristers (1810) *(page 37)*

EDWARD BIRD (1772-1819)
Signed and dated 1810
Oil on panel
62.9 x 92.7 cm
Provenance: Bought by the Prince Regent, later George IV, for 250 guineas.
First exhibited: RA 1810 (no.100) as "Village Choristers Rehearsing an Anthem for Sunday".
Literature: Oliver Millar, *The Later Georgian Pictures in the Collection of Her Majesty the Queen*, London: Phaidon, 1969, no.685. Sarah Richardson, *Edward Bird 1772-1819*, Wolverhampton: Wolverhampton Art Gallery, 1982, p.28.
Lent by Her Majesty the Queen

2

Bird trained as a japanner of teatrays in Wolverhampton, moving in about 1794 to Bristol, where he spent the remainder of his life. When his painting, *Good News*, was shown at the Royal Academy in 1809, he was hailed as a self-taught artist and a rival to David Wilkie. The rivalry with Bird undermined Wilkie's health and self-confidence: he was unable to finish *The Village Festival* in time for the Royal Academy exhibition in 1810, and was advised to withdraw *The Man with the Girl's Cap*. There may have been a political aspect to the promotion of Bird at Wilkie's expense: Bird's politics seem to have been thoroughly conservative, whereas Wilkie's were more ambiguous.[1]

Country Choristers shows villagers rehearsing an anthem for Sunday (at the same time Wilkie was working on a painting which showed them getting drunk). They are engaged, therefore, in a reassuring activity, depicted with touches of characterisation and humour which were much appreciated by contemporary observers. For example, one critic wrote:

> The subject of this Picture is supported with a great deal of propriety; the characters are happily imagined, and well distinguished, particularly those of the young man and the young woman, who form the principal groupe [sic] - There is in this groupe a degree of nature and truth, joined to a peculiar tenderness of expression, which we have seldom seen equalled - Each seems to have a respect and affection for the other; and though the young man is playing upon the flute, and the young woman singing, they seem more intent and wrapt in thought than occupied by the business before them. There is a great variety of characters introduced...and each character is finely diversified and expressed.[2]

The subject of *Country Choristers* was taken up later in the century by Webster and Hodgson (fig.14, cat.28).

1. See note 78 to Introduction; A. Cunningham, *The Life of Sir David Wilkie*, London: John Murray, 1843, I, p.287-90; Arthur S. Marks, "Rivalry at the Royal Academy: Wilkie, Turner and Bird", *Studies in Romanticism*, Vol. 20, no. 3, Fall 1981, pp.333-362.
2. *Bell's Weekly Messenger*, 20 May 1810, p.157.

3. Ale-House Politicians

**FREDERICK CHRISTIAN LEWIS, JR
(1779-1856)
after EDWARD BIRD (1772-1819)**
Mezzotint
11.2 x 15.8 cm.
Provenance: Purchased from Messrs Alais, 1868.
The British Museum

This print should be compared to Morland's *Ale-House Politicians* and Wilkie's *Village Politicians* (cats.30,45). Bird's dishevelled and unshaven figures look like dangerous ruffians, capable of revolutionary intent. As has been noted elsewhere (Introduction, note 78), Bird's work strongly suggests conservative political opinions, and his "politicians" would seem to reflect the contemporary negative stereotype of popular agitators.

The painting on which the print was based may be the *Village Politicians* shown in a Memorial Exhibition of Bird's work, Bristol 1820, described in the catalogue as "a very highly finished Cabinet Picture. We have in these figures all that effect which the art can derive from <u>contrast</u>, in the activity of the young artisan, and the repose of the old gamekeeper".[1]

3

Bird exhibited a work entitled *Politicians* at the British Institution in 1815 (no.89), but this was probably a different painting.[2] The subject matter of the present print does not quite fit the description of the work exhibited in 1820; it may be, therefore, that Bird painted at least three versions of this theme.

1. *Catalogue of Memorial Exhibition of Bird's Work*, no.37, reprinted in Sarah Richardson, "Edward Bird, R.A., 1772-1819", MPhil thesis, University of Birmingham, 1986, p.164.

2. It is described as "a slight and unpretending sketch" (*Morning Post*, 11 Feb 1815); the *Examiner* relates that it was sold to Mr Gordon, while this print is from a painting "in the collection of William Braeme Elwyn Esqre".

4. The Wife's Remonstrance (1858) *(page 39)*

JAMES CAMPBELL (c.1828-1903)
Oil on canvas
73.7 x 48.5 cm.
Provenance: McLean, Haymarket, 31 January 1885, lot 158; Sotheby's, 31 July 1957, lot 77 (as by Millais); Colnaghi; presented to the museum by the Trustees of the Feeney Charitable Trust, 1958.
First exhibited: London, Society of British Artists, 1858 (no.454).
Literature: Stephen Wildman, *Visions of Love and Life: Pre-Raphaelite Art from Birmingham Museums and Art Gallery*, Alexandria, Virginia: Art Services International, 1995, cat.45.
Birmingham Museums and Art Gallery

This painting, like others by the Pre-Raphaelites and their associates, marked a new, more realistic approach to rustic genre (see Introduction, p.9). It would have reminded contemporary viewers of a number of social issues relating to rural life: not only the issue of poaching (see Introduction, p.25-6), but also the brutalising effects of field work on women. The wife is much more masculine in appearance than the usual depictions of rural women, and her hair (and that of her daughter) is rather unkempt and greasy. All three of the figures look thin and drawn, suggesting that sacrificing the prospect of rabbit stew for supper will involve real hardship.

Campbell was a Liverpool artist, who painted a number of pictures with socially aware themes taken from modern life. John Ruskin praised *The Wife's Remonstrance* as "by far the best picture in the Suffolk Street rooms this year...full of pathos, and true painting", but chided the artist for succumbing to the fatal Pre-Raphaelite influence, "the fate of loving ugly things better than beautiful ones".

4

1. *Academy Notes*, 1858; E.T.Cook and A.Wedderburn, *The Works of John Ruskin*, London: George Allen, 1903-12, Vol.14, pp.187-8. A painting by Campbell entitled *Village Politicians* is in the Walker Art Gallery, Liverpool.

5. Sunday Morning - "La Lecture de la Bible" (c.1812) *(page 38)*

ALEXANDER CARSE (c.1770-1843)
Watercolour with gum arabic on paper
41.8 x 34.9 cm.
Provenance: Purchased 1938, from J.Kent Richardson.
Literature: L.Errington, *Alexander Carse*, c.1770-1843, National Galleries of Scotland, 1987, p.15.
National Gallery of Scotland

Alexander Carse emerged in Edinburgh during the 1790s as a draughtsman and watercolourist of topographical views: he was probably a pupil and assistant to David Allan (1744-1796). In the past this watercolour has been attributed to David Allan, although the costume and the style strongly support an

5

attribution to Carse.[1] The subject matter of his pictures is drawn from Scottish popular traditions (tent preachings, market days, tavern scenes, cotters' Saturday nights), often *via* the poetry of Burns. The style of this undated watercolour is close to that of the painting generally agreed to be his masterpiece, *The Arrival of the Country Relations* (1812; collection of the Duke of Buccleuch and Queensberry, KT). After achieving critical success in Edinburgh, he appears to have hoped to follow David Wilkie's example and make a name for himself in London. The two artists exhibited paintings of similar subjects, including illustrations to *Duncan Gray*, paintings of pedlars, and finally, in 1819, their two paintings of a *Penny Wedding* (cat.48). However, in 1820 Carse returned to Edinburgh, and the evidence suggests that his stay in London had not been a success.

This watercolour conveys an idealised view of peasant life which suggests a knowledge of the work of Greuze, presumably acquired through prints. The partly French title further confirms this influence. An elderly couple and a barefoot boy are all avidly reading the Bible, beside an open door through which sunlight streams into a barn-like interior. Such scenes usually show one person, the father of the family, reading aloud to the others: the fact that even the young boy can manage to read the Bible for himself suggests a high degree of literacy. The Scots were proud of their education system, and their network of village schools. However, the young girls do not read, implying that

their roles are more domestic. The open door, the sunlight, the boy's bare feet, and the animals who share in the mood of reverence, all suggest that a receptiveness to the precepts of the Bible is natural in humble life (see p.19, Introduction).

1. An oil painting attributed to Carse, sold at Sotheby's, Gleneagles Hotel, 25 August 1980, lot 680, contains the same group of figures, with one addition, in a more enclosed, cottage setting. (Information from the National Gallery of Scotland.)

6. The Legend (1864-78) *(page 37)*

GEORGE PAUL CHALMERS (1833-1878)
Oil on canvas
102.9 x 154.3 cm.
Provenance: said to have been commissioned by John McGavin of Glasgow, but left unfinished and unsold at Chalmers' death. Bought by the Royal Association for the Promotion of the Fine Arts in Scotland, 1878, by whom presented to the museum.
First exhibited: Royal Scottish Academy, 1879 (no.308).
Literature: Alexander Gibson and John Forbes White, *George Paul Chalmers, R.S.A.*, Edinburgh: David Douglas, 1879, pp.50-52; Edward Pinnington, *G.P.Chalmers and the Art of his Times*, Glasgow: T. and R. Annan and Sons, 1896, pp.259-66; Lindsay Errington, *Masterclass: Robert Scott Lauder and his Pupils*, Edinburgh: National Gallery of Scotland, 1983, cat.78.
Etched by Paul Adolphe Rajon for the Royal Association, 1879-80.
National Gallery of Scotland

George Paul Chalmers was an artist who was very well known in Scotland in his time, not least because of the mystery surrounding his tragic death at the age of 45.[1] However, since he rarely exhibited at the Royal Academy in London, he was comparatively unknown to the English public. *The Legend* was left unfinished when he died; he worked on it over a long period of time, and there exist a number of preparatory sketches and studies.[2] Chalmers left many pictures unfinished: he would scrape them out in a fit of despondency, and *The Legend* gave him particular difficulties. More than once his friends saw the picture looking almost complete, only to return later and find that it had been scraped out. As Lindsay Errington has observed, these drastic reworkings are evident in the slashes of paint on the dress of the child on the right.

The early biographers of Chalmers are keen to distance him from the narrative and sentimental aspects of the genre painting tradition, and stress the purely artistic problems he grappled with in *The Legend*. John Forbes White, writing in 1879, praises Chalmer's skill as a colourist. He states that, when Chalmers painted the head and sleeve of the old woman, his main influence was Rembrandt; but by the time he painted the children on the right, he was drawing his inspiration from the more subtle colourists, Turner and Velasquez. Edward Pinnington, in 1896, writes that every work of genre by Chalmers is "a work of pure art", even *The Legend*: "Do you wish to hear the old woman's story? I doubt it. Her voice is lost in the swelling harmony of colour-orchestration" (p.399).

Nevertheless, as in the case of Elizabeth Forbes (cat.20), there are interesting connections with earlier genre painting. As in the schoolroom paintings, age and youth are juxtaposed. We do not know what story the old lady is telling, but we can surmise from the facial expressions and bodily movements of the listening children that it is a gripping, mysterious or frightening one. The cottage interior, with its tiny window, looks very old and primitive, as does the old lady herself. Presumably, then, her tale is an ancient Highland legend, and the children are being instructed in the folklore traditions which are their heritage. Both Forbes and Chalmers were interested in light and colour, at a time when opinion was turning against narrative and sentiment in genre. Yet their paintings in this exhibition offer an illuminating contrast in terms of subject matter and feeling: both show women instructing children, the one in ancient, perhaps superstitious, lore, the other in rational modern education. The lighting effects on which the two painters have lavished so much attention vary accordingly, the enlightening sunlight in the Forbes painting contrasting with the mysterious smoky atmosphere in the Chalmers.

Chalmers made visits to Brittany in 1862, and to Paris and the Low Countries in 1874. He was acquainted with Jozef Israels, who also made a name for himself painting peasant genre scenes.

1. He was found with severe head injuries in an Edinburgh street, having either fallen down some steps or, as seems more likely, having been robbed and murdered. See Pinnington, pp.278-9.
2. For example: a related compositional study in the National Gallery of Scotland (D.5373); a study for the principal figure in Paisley Museum and Art Gallery; a sketch of a cottage interior in Orchar Art Gallery, Broughty Ferry; another sketch of a cottage interior, sold at Sotheby's Belgravia, 30.8.77, lot 354.

7. **Rustic Civility (1832)** *(page 40)*

WILLIAM COLLINS (1788-1847)
Oil on canvas
70.5 x 90 cm.
Provenance: Bought from the artist in 1832 by the 6th Duke of Devonshire; by descent to present owner.
First exhibited: Royal Academy, 1832 (no.29).
Literature: Wilkie Collins, *Memoirs of the Life of William Collins, Esq., R.A.*, 1848, reprinted Wakefield: E.P.Publishing, 1978, Vol II, pp.4-11; Christiana Payne, *Toil and Plenty: Images of the Agricultural Landscape in England, 1780-1890*, New Haven and London: Yale University Press, 1993, p.29-30.
Engraved: by J.Outrim; by C.Cousen.
The Duke of Devonshire and Chatsworth House Trust

This painting has become notorious as a depiction of social deference within traditional paternalistic society. However, contemporaries took it seriously, and admired it greatly both for its clever manipulation of shadows and gestures, and for its implications for national pride. The *Morning Post* (a conservative paper) gave the following description of it:

A shoeless and stockingless urchin holds a gate open by leaning against it with his back. The shadow on the ground, announcing the approach of a mounted traveller, explains the object upon which the boy's timid but respectful upward glance is fixed, as he puts his hand to his head in token of obeisance. A subject of

6

7

this kind is the test of the true pictorial spirit, and it is a test which Mr COLLINS has answered in a manner highly creditable to himself, and highly gratifying to the country which gave birth to his genius.[1]

The dates of this painting's genesis and exhibition are significant. Collins, a self-declared Tory, was working on it at the time of agitation over the Great Reform Bill; it was shown at the exhibition which coincided with the final passing of the Bill.[2] It is a depiction of the traditional landed society whose political power was directly threatened by the Bill: the "mounted traveller" is the local squire, entering the wide road which leads to his mansion and park; on the left, a narrower road leads to a farm, a symbol of the agriculture on which the gentry's wealth and power was based. The children are presumably children of the tenant farmers or labourers who work the squire's estate.

Rustic Civility exists in two versions: this is the original one, which was sold to the Duke of Devonshire. John Sheepshanks commissioned a replica, which is now in the Victoria and Albert Museum, London.

1. *Morning Post*, 9 June 1832.
2. For Collins' political views, see Wilkie Collins, *op. cit.*, Vol II, p. 3-4, 55. The Reform Bill was passed by the House of Lords on 4 June 1832 - just five days before the review quoted in this entry was published.

8. Sunday Morning (1836) (page 38)

WILLIAM COLLINS (1788-1847)
Oil on canvas
81.3 x 106.7 cm.
Provenance: Bought from the artist by George Knott for 200 guineas; Mr George Bacon of Nottingham; bequeathed to the Tate Gallery by Charles Gassiot, 1902.

that *The Poachers Alarmed* (originally called *The Poacher's Hut*) is set in Ireland. It was, apparently, this watercolour that made Fripp's reputation, since it attracted "warm and abundant praises from artists of all sorts" (H.S.Thompson, *op.cit.*)

The theme of poaching has been discussed in the Introduction (p.25-6). Fripp's watercolour stresses the dangers involved, and is thus a reminder of the harshness of the Game Laws. As one critic noted, the composition is reminiscent of Wilkie's *Peep'o'Day Boy's Cabin* (fig.15):

> In the <u>Poacher's Hut</u> Mr A.Fripp rises to a higher ambition, daring to measure himself against Wilkie; since, who that sees the work under notice will forget <u>The Peep of Day Boy's Cabin</u>? Here is the same arrangement: the man sleeping off his labour - the woman watching at his side (what an epitome, by the way, of the two lives!). But we are not sure that the Royal Academician himself rendered the intensity of apprehensiveness better than the humble watercolourist has done, in the listening head and the gleaming eye-ball of the female figure. There is considerable vigour in this drawing. [1]

The contrast between the man and the woman is paralleled, too, in James Campbell's later painting, *The Wife's Remonstrance* (cat.4).

1. *Athenaeum*, 4 May 1844, p.411.

22. **Preparing for Dinner (1854)** *(page 45)*

FREDERICK DANIEL HARDY (1826-1911)
Signed F.D.H. and dated 1854
Oil on panel
22 x 33 cm.
Provenance: Sidney Cartwright; Cartwright Bequest to museum, 1887.
Wolverhampton Art Gallery Collection

This exquisitely painted cottage interior is very typical of Hardy's early work. Drawing on sources in Dutch art and perhaps also on Chardin (see Introduction, p.13) he concentrates on homely settings: cottages with brick walls and floors, wooden beams, simple furniture, ancient fireplaces and utensils. The pervading atmosphere is one of tranquillity and delight in simple pleasures (see also Introduction, p.10). The figures are themselves treated almost like still life, attractive objects for the light to fall on. In this case they also illustrate typical cottage virtues. The grandmother, in the room beyond, has fallen asleep over her knitting; a large book, probably the Bible, lies on the table and there is a spinning wheel beside her. In the foreground, the mother peeling carrots is watched by the child, who learns from her example. The values of industry, piety and education are presented in a way that is subtle, appealing and not obviously didactic.

21

23. Expectation: Interior of a Cottage with a Mother and Children (1854)

(page 45)

FREDERICK DANIEL HARDY (1826-1911)
Oil on panel
22.8 x 30.4 cm.
Provenance: Samuel Mayou of Birmingham; his sale, Christie's, 21 April 1883 (lot 19) as *Interior of a Cottage with a Mother and Children*; bought Martin £99.15s on behalf of Thomas Holloway.
First exhibited: Royal Academy 1854 (no.505), as "Expectation".
Literature: Jeannie Chapel, *Victorian Taste: the Complete Catalogue of Paintings at the Royal Holloway College*, A.Zwemmer Ltd, 1982, cat.26.
Royal Holloway College, University of London

This painting focuses on the virtues of motherhood, widely considered to be seen at their best in a rural setting. The mother feeds her baby with help from the older girl, who is already showing the qualities which will make her a good mother in her turn. Behind them, the darkness of the fireplace is relieved by a small window (perhaps the result of artistic licence) in which a plant grows. The analogy between healthy, well-tended plants and sympathetically brought-up children was often suggested in cottage interiors.

24. The Dismayed Artist (1866) *(page 46)*

FREDERICK DANIEL HARDY (1826-1911)
Signed and dated F.D.Hardy, Cranbrook, 1866
Oil on panel
46 x 61.5 cm.
Provenance: Sidney Cartwright; Cartwright Bequest to Museum, 1887.
First exhibited: RA 1866 (no.433).
Literature: Andrew Greg, *The Cranbrook Colony*, catalogue of exhibition at Vestry Hall, Cranbrook, 1981, p.20.
Wolverhampton Art Gallery Collection

This painting, which may be based on an actual incident that occurred in Cranbrook, dramatises the contrast between the artist's attitude to picturesque cottages and the more practical approach of those who actually lived in them. Hardy has arrived at a cottage, accompanied by his brother George, in order to continue work on a study of the fireplace, which he holds in his hand. However, he is horrified to find the housewife and her children whitewashing the old bricks that he has been transcribing so carefully onto his canvas. His easel and paintbox occupy the left foreground: the label on the paintbox acts as a signature, while the label on the easel, "Chari(ng Cross) to Staplehu(rst)" is a further reminder that the art world is based in London, where attitudes are very different from those of the countryside.

22

23

24

The theme of the gulf between middle-class, artistic expectations and the true interests of the rural poor was a common one in the mid-nineteenth century. John Ruskin and George Eliot stressed the heartlessness of picturesque theory, which ignored the practical disadvantages of dirt, decay and rags, and only saw their pictorial value.[1] A comment by a reviewer on a picture by Mark Anthony, *The Pedlar's Visit to an Old Cottage* (1860) is typical: "The building...is of the class which looks very well in pictures, but that forms very indifferent habitations."[2] Whitewashing brick would have several practical advantages: it would reduce the dust from the bricks, make them easier to keep clean, and make the room brighter. Hardy presumably realised this, and his picture pokes fun at artistic sensibilities, depicting himself and his brother as effete aesthetes, in contrast to the down-to-earth cottage housewife and her sturdy children.

1. J.Ruskin, *Modern Painters*, Vol. 4 (E.T.Cook and A.Wedderburn, eds., *The Works of John Ruskin*, London: George Allen, 1903-12, Vol.VI, p.19-22). Ruskin characterises the lover of the picturesque as "heartless" and "merciless", delighting in the sight of disorder and ruin, although he goes on to say that the love of the picturesque leads to a truer sympathy with the poor and a better understanding of the right ways of helping them. George Eliot satirises "that softening influence of the fine arts which makes other people's hardships picturesque" in *Middlemarch*, first published 1872 (London: Zodiac Press, 1967, p.378).
2. *Art Journal*, 1860, p.80.

25. A Schule Skailin' (1846) (page 42)

SIR GEORGE HARVEY (1806-1876)
Signed
Oil on panel
69.3 x 120.7 cm.
Provenance: Drysdale Carstairs, Esq., 1850; Duncan J. Kay, 1901; presented to National Gallery of Scotland by Mrs Duncan J. Kay, 1904.
First exhibited: Royal Scottish Academy, 1846 (no 63).
Literature: Smith Art Gallery, Stirling, *Paintings and Drawings by Sir George Harvey*, 1985.
Engraved: by William Howison.
National Gallery of Scotland
(Nottingham only)

Harvey exhibited a painting of a village school at the Institution, Edinburgh in 1826; it is probable that his interest in the subject arose as a result of knowledge of Wilkie's *Village School* (fig.4), which dates from the early 1820s. *A Schule Skailin'* has certain features in common with Wilkie's version, such as the contrast between the subdued girls and the boisterous boys, and the appearance of the schoolmaster. Unlike Mulready's *The Last In* (cat.31), Harvey's schoolroom is a purpose-built one, with desks and benches along the side walls.

25

In the archives of the National Gallery of Scotland, there is a letter to the artist from James Chrystal of Stirling (a fellow artist), dated 15 January 1846, which provides a valuable insight into the way these schoolroom paintings were regarded by their contemporary audience.

> I congratulate you upon the success of the happy boys just let out to play (See Goldsmith).[1] The Dominie and his scanty scratch wig, I have still before me. An old industrious man commanding respect mingled with sympathy. Happy in his own attainments, and the highest in his humble sphere being the rules governing relative prepositions, in syntax, those of vulgar fractions in arithmetic, and reciting in a shaky voice Adam's address to Eve! followed with a self approving harl of snuff from a bone spoon...The contrast between the staid quietness of old age and the boisterous mirth of youth is to me, quite overcoming....
>
> Allow one to suggest for your consideration giving the name to the painting of "The School Skailing" - The subject is Scotch - and to whose recollection of boyhood and mischief, are these...words not electrical? They are talismanic. They are co-eval with the bools - the pirie - The shorter catechism and cudgels - the bible - sweeties and blackman - crusht therein - the dabbing book - halvers in buttons, a feight to be between lang stink and toom breeks. Scotch and English, hyspys - etc etc...& squibs bought & let off in stealth and ultimately the persecution of some decent auld wifes cat - or the spoiling of Nancy Gilmours grozerts which she had lain upon all night to ripen. Excuse this nonsense but the recollections called up by your picture are delightful.

The research of Lindsay Errington has explained many of the terms in this remarkable letter; others remain mysterious. Bools are marbles, a pirie is a top, blackman is liquorice, halvers in buttons are sharers in the game of buttons aimed at a mark, hyspys is I-spy. The "feight to be between lang stink and toom breeks" refers to the fight between Longshanks (King Edward of England) and Toom Tabard (John Balliol of Scotland).[2] The word "skailing" means scattering.

In Scotland, the village schools catered for a much wider social range than their equivalents in England, and so many well-off exhibition visitors would have related them to their own childhoods. The Goldsmith reference, and the recollection by Chrystal of his own childhood, may indicate that the scene is meant to be set in the past.

The picture was shown again at the Royal Academy in 1871, and went to the Universal Exhibition in Vienna in 1873. The National Gallery of Scotland has letters and telegrams from Thomas Faed, Fred Barwell, Francis Grant and Erskine Nicol, all expressing their admiration for the picture at this period.

1. Oliver Goldsmith - *The Deserted Village* (1770) - "The playful children just let loose from school" are part of the sights and sounds of village before enclosure (line 120).
2. Notes on the picture in the archives of the National Gallery of Scotland.

26. The Invalid (c.1889) (page 39)

JAMES HAYLLAR (1829-1920)
Signed
Oil on canvas
91.4 x 63.5 cm.
Provenance: Given to museum by P.W.Gunsaker, 1968.
First exhibited: Possibly Society of British Artists, 1889 (no.355), as "An Easy Chair for his Old Woman".
Literature: Christopher Wood, "The Artistic Family Hayllar: Part One: James Hayllar", *Connoisseur*, April 1974, pp.266-73.
City of Nottingham Museums; Castle Museum and Art Gallery

James Hayllar exhibited at the Royal Academy and at the Society of British Artists for over 40 years, and he also trained his four daughters, Jessica, Edith, Mary and Kate, as painters.[1] From 1875 the family rented a large house, Castle Priory, on the banks of the Thames at Wallingford. James Hayllar produced many finely detailed paintings of rustic life, using models from amongst the local villagers. *The Invalid* is similar to photographs of rustic life of the late nineteenth-century in its concentration on old people, who continue to wear picturesque smocks and represent the continuity of old habits at a time when country life was changing rapidly. If *The Invalid* is the painting exhibited in 1889 as "An Easy Chair for his Old Woman", then the title draws attention to the beautifully worked patchwork chair - which is, indeed, unusually fine for a cottage interior. The implication

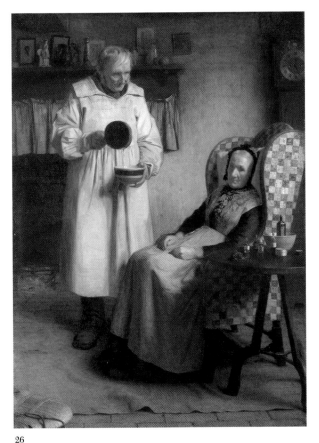

26

First exhibited: Society of Painters in Watercolour, 1810 (no.86).
Literature: William T.Whitley, *Thomas Heaphy (1775-1835), First President of the Society of British Artists*, Royal Society of British Artists' Art Club Publications no.1, 1933; Hesketh Hubbard, *Thomas Heaphy (1775-1835)*, Old Water-Colour Society's Club, 26th Annual Volume, 1948, ed. Adrian Bury, p.19-30.
Laing Art Gallery, Newcastle upon Tyne (Tyne and Wear Museums)

Thomas Heaphy had great success with his genre paintings in the first decade of the nineteenth century. Buyers of his watercolours included Sir Thomas Lawrence, the Marquis of Stafford and Sir William Watkins Wynne. However, he was criticised for his low and vulgar subjects and their dubious morality; some of his pictures show rustic characters committing robbery and apparently getting away with it.

A Fisherman's Cottage, however, depicts a poor family behaving in an exemplary way. Mother and father show devotion to their little ones, and the grandmother has been reading the family Bible, in which the marriage of the couple and the birthdates of their children are recorded. The Bible is in a state of dilapidation which suggests that it is read constantly: it is open at the book of Isaiah, Chapter LIII. The mother breastfeeding the baby, and the cottage which seems to open directly onto a beach, extol the virtues of a life lived close to nature. Like Carse's *Sunday Morning* (cat.5) this watercolour appears to show the artistic influence of Greuze and, in general terms, that of the ideas of Jean-Jacques Rousseau (see Introduction, p.23).

may be that it is a gift from a well-to-do visitor, making this painting another variation on the theme of charity.

The old lady turns away from the light, suggesting that she is soon to die, even though it is springtime, as indicated by the bunch of violets on the table next to her medicines. Her pallor is poignantly contrasted with the ruddy cheeks of the old man. The mood of the picture is peaceful rather than gloomy, suggesting the conclusion of a life which, while hardworking, has been virtuous and satisfying.

1. C.Wood, "The Artistic Family Hayllar: Part Two: Jessica, Edith, Mary and Kate", *Connoisseur*, May 1974, pp.2-9.

27. A Fisherman's Cottage (1810) *(page 47)*

THOMAS HEAPHY (1775-1835)
Signed and dated 1810.
Watercolour on paper
47.4 x 62.9 cm.
Provenance: Walker Galleries, 1929; bought by Walker Mechanics Institute (Newcastle upon Tyne), 1930 (Trustees of John Wigham Richardson Bequest), and given by them to the museum.

27

In 1810 Heaphy had eight exhibits at the Society of Painters in Watercolour. He sold four of them for a total of 520 guineas (Hesketh Hubbard, *op.cit.*, p.25); this one appears to have remained unsold. David Wilkie went to see the exhibition and recorded his admiration for Heaphy in his diary: "the industry of the latter [Heaphy] is beyond all example. When I think of the number of highly finished objects which he has in those pictures of his, and compare them with what I myself have done in the same time, my labour seems idleness. I must exert myself more."[1]

1. A.Cunningham, *The Life of Sir David Wilkie*, London: John Murray, 1843, Vol.I p.298.

28

28. A Philharmonic Rehearsal in a Farmhouse (1860) *(page 46)*

JOHN EVAN HODGSON (1831-95)
Signed and dated 1860
Oil on canvas
86.5 x 112 cm.
Provenance: Sidney Cartwright; Cartwright Bequest to museum, 1887.
First exhibited: Royal Academy 1860 (no.596), as "Our Philharmonic Society at its first rehearsal".
Literature: Gail-Nina Anderson and Joanne Wright, *The Pursuit of Leisure: Victorian Depictions of Pastimes*, Nottingham: Djanogly Art Gallery in association with Lund Humphries, 1997, cat. 70.

Wolverhampton Art Gallery Collection
(Nottingham only)

Hodgson was born in London, but was brought up in Russia where his father was in business. He entered the Royal Academy schools as a student in

1855, and mainly painted historical and Arab subjects; he did, however, paint a few pictures of country life with topical and somewhat humorous themes.[1] His *Philharmonic Rehearsal* is derived in part from Thomas Webster's *Village Choir* (fig.14), especially in its contrast of villagers of different social status. The man with the cello evidently thinks himself superior to the rest, while the bearded man at the window, with his smartly dressed child, looks uncomfortable in these rustic surroundings. The setting is probably the home of a village craftsman, rather than a farmhouse: the present title (which is not Hodgson's own) is rather misleading. Hodgson's own title suggests that the artist is a resident of the village, who has joined in one of its communal activities and is sharply aware of the social distinctions which made such ventures perilous.

There are many indications of social progress in this rustic interior. The old virtues are still practised - the grandfather, for example, has his seat by the fire, both parents are attentive to their children - but other features are modern. The daughter is being reproved for getting ink on her pinafore from her school work; this, then, is a household where education and literacy are making an impact. Still life objects indicate that the family is affected by the fashionable mania for collecting shells, fossils and stuffed animals. The ammonite set into the floor, next to the shuttlecock, a traditional vanitas symbol, contrasts the vastness of geological time with the brevity of human life, a common theme of this period (the painting was exhibited one year after Charles Darwin's *The Origin of Species* was published).

1. For example, *The Farmer's Dream*, illustrated in C. Wood, *Paradise Lost: Paintings of English Country Life and Landscape, 1850-1914*, London: Barrie and Jenkins, 1988, p.36; and an intriguing picture entitled 'Elector and Candidate - "Are we not Brothers?" ' (1858), sold at Christie's, London, 5 June 1981, lot 78. The latter shows a Parliamentary candidate talking to a carpenter in his workshop, while the carpenter's wife and baby look on.

29. Interior of a Highlander's House (c.1831) *(page 47)*

SIR EDWIN LANDSEER (1802-1873)
Oil on panel
69.8 x 85 cm.
Provenance: William Wells of Redleaf; Wells sale, Christie's, 10 May 1890, lot 32; Lord Masham; by descent to the Countess of Swinton; sold from Swinton House, Christie's, 21 November 1975, lot 74, and 19 February 1979, lot 21.

First exhibited: Royal Academy, 1831 (no.86).
Literature: R.Ormond, *Sir Edwin Landseer*,
London: Thames and Hudson in association with
Philadelphia Museum of Art and the Tate
Gallery, 1981, p.77.
Engraved: by Finden, 1839.
Private Collection
(Not exhibited)

The London-born Sir Edwin Landseer is best known as a sporting and animal painter, but between 1830 and 1834 he exhibited seven pictures of Highland interiors. He first went to the Highlands, where his patron, the Duke of Bedford, had a hunting lodge, in 1824; thereafter he made visits every autumn, both for the hunting and in search of subjects for his painting. The novels of Sir Walter Scott contributed to the popularity of the Highlands at this period.

Richard Ormond identifies this interior as the home of a ghillie, or hunter's attendant, and points out how "the beautifully painted earthenware bowl and jar on the left, the bunch of heather, the kippers hanging over the stove, and the Bible on the dresser suggest a simple and well-ordered existence." At the same Royal Academy exhibition in 1831, Landseer also showed *The Poacher's Bothy* (Hamburger, Kunsthalle). Taken together, these two paintings contrast the domestic contentment of the ghillie, who has got his game legally, with the desperate life of the poacher, who lives in constant fear of detection and has none of the domestic comforts enjoyed by the ghillie.

29

Two other well-known pictures by Landseer, *A Highland Breakfast* (1834, Victoria and Albert Museum, London) and *The Old Shepherd's Chief Mourner* (1837, Victoria and Albert Museum) also celebrate the domestic virtues of Highland cottagers.

30. Ale-House Politicians

WILLIAM WARD (1766-1826)
after GEORGE MORLAND (1763-1804)
Mezzotint
45 x 60 cm.
Provenance: not known.
The British Museum

This print may well have suggested to Wilkie the subject of *The Village Politicians* (cat.45). A man reads aloud from the *Sun* - a conservative newspaper. The portraits of soldiers on the walls suggest that this is a patriotic establishment, and not one where radical politics would be discussed. On the other hand, the mood is serious and Morland certainly does not seem to wish to ridicule the idea of tradesmen taking an interest in politics. The three men on the left all look at the newspaper, while the shepherd, with his smock and crook (who may be illiterate) stands somewhat aloof from the group. The man seated in front of the table to the left has an awl attached to his apron, showing that he is a cobbler, an occupation often associated with radical politics.

Morland's biographer, John Hassell, wrote of this print:

> This is exceedingly well engraved, but it is too low a subject to merit the same attention as several other pictures of this artist, who gave himself a latitude upon some occasions, that was very disgusting to a man of taste.[1]

As John Barrell has shown, Morland's biographers were quick to criticise any works by Morland which suggested that the peasantry were idle or politically conscious. Such subject matter had to be carefully negotiated if it was to meet with approval from patrons and critics.

1. J. Hassell, *Memoirs of the Life of George Morland*, London, 1806, p.154. Most of this is quoted by John Barrell in *The Dark Side of the Landscape: the Rural Poor in English Painting, 1730-1840*, Cambridge: Cambridge University Press, 1980, p.102.

30

31. The Last In (1835) *(page 44)*

WILLIAM MULREADY (1786-1863)

Oil on panel

62.2 x 76.2 cm.

Provenance: Robert Vernon, by whom given to National Gallery, 1847.

First exhibited: Royal Academy, 1835 (no.105).

Literature: K.M. Heleniak, *William Mulready*, Yale University Press, 1980, cat. no. 144, pp.85-6; M.Pointon, *Mulready*, Victoria and Albert Museum, 1986, pp.100-101; Robin Hamlyn, *Robert Vernon's Gift: British Art for the Nation, 1847*, London: Tate Gallery, 1993, cat. 50.

Engraved: by J.T.Smyth, *Art Journal*, 1850, facing p.76.

Tate Gallery

The artistic sources, narrative and characterisation of this painting, and its relationship to educational reforms, have been discussed in the Introduction, pp.9 and 24-5. Mulready would have been exposed to progressive ideas on education in the circle of William Godwin, for whom he worked in his youth, and these are probably the source for his contrast between the prison-like school and the idyllic landscape outside. The painting also shows the influence of Wilkie's *Village School* (fig.4). In both works, lively boys are contrasted with docile, attentive girls, and there is a specific borrowing in the girl on the right who looks at the observer from behind her book. At this stage in his career Mulready was painting in pure colours over a white ground - a parallel to fresco technique - and the colours, as well as some of the figures, are reminiscent of Raphael's fresco *The School at Athens*.

Mulready made small drawings of individual figures for the painting (cats.35,36) as well as a full-scale cartoon (cat.34). He seems to have been aiming not so much at realism as at an overall effect of harmony and beauty: the clothes of the late boy flow smoothly, like Biblical draperies, and the girl in white who looks across at him in sympathy, her hand pointing towards her heart, has the grace of a Renaissance saint.

38

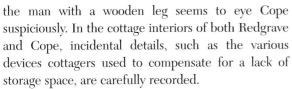

39

the man with a wooden leg seems to eye Cope suspiciously. In the cottage interiors of both Redgrave and Cope, incidental details, such as the various devices cottagers used to compensate for a lack of storage space, are carefully recorded.

39. Study for Boy leaning on a Stile (c.1846)

RICHARD REDGRAVE (1804-1888)
pencil and bodycolour on paper
26.7 x 14.6 cm.
Provenance: Given to the museum by the family of Richard Redgrave.
Literature: S. Casteras and R. Parkinson, eds., *Richard Redgrave 1804-1888*, New Haven and London: Yale University Press in association with the Victoria and Albert Museum and the Yale Center for British Art, 1988, cat.59.
The Board of Trustees of the Victoria and Albert Museum, London

This is a study, presumably done from a model in the studio, for a figure in Redgrave's painting, *Sunday Morning, the Walk from Church* (fig.22). Redgrave's careful draughtsmanship is comparable to that of Wilkie, Mulready and Cope, all of whom made meticulous studies for their rustic genre paintings.

In the painting, the boy is separated from the group going home after church, perhaps indicating that he is unable to attend church because he is too poor and lacks suitable clothes. However, he holds a book and points to it, to show that he can still read prayers while he tends his sheep.

Fig.22 Richard Redgrave, *Sunday Morning, the Walk from Church*, 1846. Oil on Canvas, 71.1 x 110.8 cm. Private Collection.

40. The Poacher's Home (c.1868) *(page 48)*

THOMAS WADE (1828-1891)
Signed with monogram
Oil on canvas
42.8 x 33.5 cm.
Provenance: Bought by museum from Mrs H.Richardson, 1940.
First exhibited: Royal Academy 1868 (no.218).
Literature: Exhibition leaflet, *Thomas Wade: Preston's Pre-Raphaelite*, Harris Museum and Art Gallery, Preston.
Harris Museum and Art Gallery, Preston

Thomas Wade's small paintings are perhaps the closest any British artist of this period came to social realism in the depiction of the English cottage interior. The details of his training as an artist are unknown;

40

41

he lived in Preston, sending paintings from there to the Royal Academy from 1867 until 1890; after 1879 he moved to Windermere. *Carting Turf from the Moss* (Harris Museum and Art Gallery, Preston), his best-known painting, was shown at the Royal Academy in 1867. Presumably influenced by the Pre-Raphaelites, he produced a series of genre scenes and landscapes which are remarkable for their truthfulness and their acceptance of the harsher side of rural life. Unlike so many spacious cottage interiors, *The Poacher's Home* is cramped and overcrowded: the children huddle in front of the fire, preparing the evening meal, while the poacher looks towards the door, perhaps fearing detection. There is no mother in evidence: she may be out at work or dead, and the eldest daughter has to take on her role as housewife.

41. A Stitch in Time (c.1868) *(page 48)*

THOMAS WADE (1828-1891)
Signed with monogram
Oil on panel
53.3 x 35.5 cm.
Provenance: Bought by museum from Dr and Mrs Richardson, 1935.
First exhibited: Royal Academy 1868 (no.420).
Literature: Exhibition leaflet, *Thomas Wade: Preston's Pre-Raphaelite*, Harris Museum and Art Gallery, Preston.
Harris Museum and Art Gallery, Preston

See the entry for no.40. This painting shows the home of a weaver, who is seen hard at work in the background. The hard-pressed mother attempts to spin, look after a baby (who is in danger of falling off her lap) and attend to an older daughter, all at the same time. Thus, although she embodies some of the cherished cottage virtues, she is also a reminder of the hardships of working-class life, in contrast to the peaceful, serene existence conveyed by the mothers and children in cottage scenes by Frederick Daniel Hardy (cats.22 and 23).

42. Good Night! (1846) *(page 49)*

THOMAS WEBSTER (1800-1886)
Oil on panel
71.4 x 118.7 cm
Provenance: Duncan Fletcher; Elhanan Bicknell sale, Christie's 25 April 1863, sold for 1160

guineas; sold Christie's 20 May 1865, bt. Vokins, 865 guineas; Ralph Brocklebank, 1866; Frost and Reed, 1957, from whom purchased by museum.

First exhibited: Royal Academy, 1846 (no.417), with quotation: "the little strong embrace of prattling children twined around his neck, etc." Literature: Christiana Payne, *Toil and Plenty: Images of the Agricultural Landscape in England, 1780-1890*, New Haven and London: Yale University Press, 1993, pp.34-5; "Rural Virtues for Urban Consumption: Cottage Scenes in Early Victorian Painting", *Journal of Victorian Culture*, 3.1, Spring 1998, pp.51-4, 62.

Bristol Museums and Art Gallery

As the review quoted on p.18 of the Introduction indicates, this painting sums up the ideal of happy cottage life: blest contentment joined with honest labour. The reviewer went on to pick out "the merry children", "the expectant look of the hoary veteran", "the affection that beams through the cheerful countenance of the father" as "felicitous touches of nature"; and also drew particular attention to the grandmother who "listens to the prayer that she has taught". The devotion of each member of the family to the others is skilfully portrayed. The old people are well looked after, occupying honoured places by the fire or at the head of the table; the children are shown growing up to espouse their parents' virtues, praying, helping with their smaller brothers and sisters, or awaiting their meal after a day's labour. Still life details, too, are carefully manipulated to emphasize this family's thrift and cleanliness: the bowl of amazingly clean water, complete with soap and a sponge; the neatly made

42

bed, visible in the room beyond. Both details related to contemporary concerns about working-class housing, especially the lack of pure water which led to disease and the cramped sleeping quarters which were blamed for promiscuity and even incest (see Introduction, p.26-7).

The interior is a spacious one, perhaps too spacious to be the residence of a labourer. However, if the man is a farmer, he is a hard-working one, without social pretensions. The sickle, the boy's smock, and the beer keg in front of the dog indicate that the three men of the family have been out working in the fields, probably harvesting. The cottage and its furnishings are plain but well cared for (the floor of brick and wood is chipped, but well scrubbed). Evening sunlight streams in from the open window, picking out important details such as happy faces, the hands of the grandfather, the bowl of water, sparkling crockery, and the bed in the background.

In 1887, a younger rustic genre painter, John Evan Hodgson (cat.28), gave an analysis of Webster's work which neatly illustrates the change in attitudes towards rural virtue in the later decades of the nineteenth century. He states that he knew Webster as a kindly old man, who "had a spirit of extreme purity and kindliness, of sincere love for the humble virtues and simple joys which he depicted; his belief in them is a standing rebuke to the irreverent cynicism in which we have all been brought up". He continued:

> On the evidence of Webster's pictures, we feel inclined to accept the fact, that there was a period in English history - a not very remote one either - when the agricultural labourer was satisfied with his lot, and did not quarrel with his employer about his wages - when he did not spend these in the public-house, to the detriment of his family, when he was content to live at home and enjoy the frugal blessings which were graced by the lustre of the paternal salt-cellar. Webster's peasants...belong to an ideal world, but it is a beautiful one, and his art has a neatness and precision, a limpid translucent quality of colour which is in strict keeping with the nature of the conception, and seems in an equal degree to minister to the soul's needs.[1]

1. J.E.Hodgson, R.A., *Fifty Years of British Art, as Illustrated by the Pictures and Drawings in the Manchester Royal Jubilee Exhibition*, London and Manchester: John Heywood, 1887, p.18.

44. Card Players (1848 or later)

LUMB STOCKS (1812-1892)
after THOMAS WEBSTER (1800-1886)
Engraving
50.3 x 41.6 cm.
Provenance: Purchased from W.Holloway, 1853.
The British Museum

Scenes of rustics playing cards were popular with seventeenth-century genre painters; since Wilkie's *Card Players* of 1807 (Lord Denham)[1] British artists had used the theme to convey subtle psychological relationships and expressions. This print is based on a painting by Webster, shown at the Royal Academy in 1848, no. 176. (Untraced, but a photograph in the Witt Library, Courtauld Institute records it as being in the collection of Mrs H.B.Brown, decd, Chester.) The critic of the *Athenaeum* was highly approving:

> Since the days when Wilkie discontinued the illustration of scenes of domestic life we have had no one to succeed him in that class until Mr Webster appeared. In his interior, <u>A Rubber</u> (176), he has taken a high stand - conveying in it proof of the extent and subtlety of his observation. The stolid, nay stupid, perplexity of the countryman who, on the left, is puzzled what to lead is full of eloquence - while his partner regards him with the keen apprehension and distrust that denote the sharp reproof to follow the mistake which he is sure to make. The happy and confident expression of the sturdy and sleek old yeoman who anticipates the card about to be led, and will finesse with all the certainty which his excellent hand prompts - and the responsive air of his <u>vis-a-vis</u>, the youngest of the party, who awaits with security his turn to gain the trick - are all told. In every head and in every gesture may the story be followed with as much clearness as if set down in written definition.[2]

The engraver, Lumb Stocks, has paid great attention to these qualities of character and expression, as well as to the effects of sunlight streaming in from the open window. The old man seems to have been used by Webster again as a model for the father in his *Letter from the Colonies* (1852; Tate Gallery, London).

43

43. A Tea Party (1862) (page 49)

THOMAS WEBSTER (1800-1886)
Signed and dated 1862
Oil on panel
50.8 x 61 cm.
Provenance: Painted for Richard Newsham;
Richard Newsham Bequest to museum, 1883.
First Exhibited: Royal Academy 1863 (no.159).
Literature: Agnews, *Victorian Painting 1837-1887*, 1961, no.85.
Harris Museum and Art Gallery, Preston

Compared to *Good Night!* (cat.42), this shows a more prosperous interior, with children playing at being adults, rather than saying their prayers before bedtime. Webster's later cottage interiors are less rustic and closer to middle-class life. Although, by this stage of his career, he was living in Cranbrook and painting in the local cottages, he seems deliberately to have sought out the more spacious cottages or farmhouses, conveying a reassuring vision of the prosperity of rural life in Kent. The large window with its net curtain suggests a farmhouse rather than a cottage, and the children are well dressed and have a good selection of toys. Like *Good Night!*, this painting shows the grandmother performing a useful function, looking after the children while their parents are at work.

44

The different clothes of the participants in the card game signify their varying occupations and social status: the smock of a labourer, the apron of an artisan, the striped coat of the "yeoman". The man on the right, wearing a long coat, seems to be of a higher status, and his discomfiture contributes to the humour of the work: similar effects are found in Webster's *Village Choir* (fig.14) and Hodgson's *Philharmonic Rehearsal* (cat.28).

1. See Hamish Miles, *Sir David Wilkie*, London: Richard L.Feigen and company, 1994, no.6.
2. *Athenaeum*, 6 May 1848, p.464.

45. The Village Politicians (1805) (page 50)

SIR DAVID WILKIE (1785-1841)
Oil on canvas
57.2 x 75 cm.
Provenance: Bought from the artist by the Earl of Mansfield; by descent to the present owner.
First exhibited: Royal Academy 1806 (no.145).
Literature: Lindsay Errington, *Tribute to Wilkie*, Edinburgh: National Galleries of Scotland, 1985, pp.29-30; Duncan Macmillan, *Painting in Scotland: the Golden Age*, Oxford: Phaidon Press, 1986, p.162; Hamish Miles, *Sir David Wilkie 1785-1841*, London: Richard L.Feigen and Company, 1994, cat.4.
Engraved: by Abraham Raimbach, 1814.
The Earl of Mansfield, Scone Palace

The Village Politicians was Wilkie's first big success. Lord Mulgrave and Sir George Beaumont went to see the painting and were so impressed that they immediately gave Wilkie commissions; their influence ensured that it was hung in a favourable position at the Royal Academy exhibition of 1806, where it is said to have attracted huge crowds. Its success can be attributed partly to its relationship to seventeenth-century sources (see Introduction, p.11-12), partly to its topicality at a time when debates over Parliamentary reform were beginning to become important, and memories of the unrest of the 1790s were still fresh in people's minds (p.24).

In the Academy catalogue, Wilkie referred his viewers to "Scotland's Skaith" a poem by Hector MacNeill, which warned of the dire consequences that came from reading Jacobinical papers, such as the *Gazeteer*, in alehouses. However, the painting draws on a wide range of sources, both visual and literary. The arrangement of the participants in a debate is like

Hannah More's *Village Politics*, 1793, which is written as a dialogue between Jack Anvil the blacksmith and Tom Hod the mason. This was a counter-revolutionary tract: Jack has been reading the *Rights of Man*, and wants liberty and happiness like they have in France; but Tom manages to convince him that the Bible is a more trustworthy source of ideas, and that the poor depend on the rich for work and charity. This pamphlet, ostensibly by "Will Chip, a country carpenter" was reissued at times when public disturbances threatened, and its efficacy was widely recognised.[1]

The closest artistic precedent for Wilkie's painting was George Morland's *Ale-House Politicians* (cat.30). Morland's rustics have a serious mood, which is more challenging politically than Wilkie's humorous treatment (admittedly, they are reading a conservative paper, *The Sun*, but they could well be disagreeing with its arguments). Conservative critics were able to find in Wilkie's painting confirmation of their beliefs about the incapability of the lower classes to make an informed contribution to political debate. *La Belle Assemblée*, for example, regarded the two main figures as "admirably characteristic of the conceit which a little knowledge produces on vulgar minds".[2] However, the painting was also open to interpretations sympathetic to democracy, and, as well as the conservatives, Mulgrave and Beaumont, one of the patrons who was attracted to Wilkie by it was Samuel Whitbread, the prominent radical. Later on, the anonymous writer of the text to a collection of prints after Wilkie, *The Wilkie Gallery*, interpreted the man on the left as an "ardent young ploughman, intoxicated with the new light of liberalism" and "deaf to the clamorous exceptions of his antagonists".[3] According to their own political sympathies, in other words, observers could decide which of Wilkie's characters held the most radical views, and which side was winning the argument.

Prints after *The Village Politicians* had a great influence in Germany, and also in America, where the subject appears to have been seen as especially suitable for an emerging democracy.[4]

1. See R.K.Webb, *The British Working Class Reader, 1790-1848: Literacy and Social Tension*, New York: Augustus M.Kelley, 1955, reprinted 1971, p.42ff.
2. *La Belle Assemblée, or, Bell's Court and Fashionable Magazine, addressed particularly to the Ladies*, London: J.Bell, 1806, p.216.
3. *The Wilkie Gallery. A Selection of the best pictures of the late Sir David Wilkie, R.A.*, London: George Virtue, 1851, p.14.
4. Arthur S.Marks, "Wilkie and the Reproductive Print", in H.A.D.Miles et al., *Sir David Wilkie of Scotland*, Raleigh: North Carolina Museum of Art, 1987, pp.93-4.

45

46

Fig.23 Thomas Heaphy, *The Village Doctress*, 1809.
Watercolour on Paper, 48.3 x 62.2 cm. V&A Picture Library.

46. The Cut Finger (1809) (page 50)

SIR DAVID WILKIE (1785-1841)
Oil on panel
34.3 x 46 cm.
Provenance: Bought by Samuel Whitbread II in 1809, thence by descent to present owner.
First exhibited: Royal Academy 1809 (no.123).
Literature: S.Deuchar, *Paintings, Politics and Porter: Samuel Whitbread II (1764-1815) and British Art*, London: Whitbread & Co for the Museum of London, 1984, cat.67; H.A.D.Miles et al., *Sir David Wilkie of Scotland*, Raleigh: North Carolina Museum of Art, 1987, cat.11.
Engraved: by Abraham Raimbach, 1813.
Private Collection
(Nottingham only)

Many of Wilkie's patrons were conservative politicians; however, for a short period he worked for Samuel Whitbread II, a noted radical who advocated a statutory minimum wage for farm labourers, championed the establishment of universal education and opposed the continuation of the war with France. Whitbread came to see Wilkie after the exhibition of *The Village Politicians* (cat.45), *The Cut Finger* was painted for him, and Wilkie went to stay at Whitbread's house at Southill Park. Whitbread was one of the earliest Englishmen to announce his intention of forming a gallery of British art.[1]

Wilkie's biographer, Allan Cunningham, says that Whitbread originally decided to call the picture *The Young Navigator*, desiring "to see in its story the maritime glory of England in the dawn", but Stephen Deuchar suggests that Whitbread would have been more likely to see it as a warning to Britain to avoid naval aggression. The little boy, as Cunningham points out, is not a very good advertisement for the British navy, since he is hardly stoical in the face of his self-inflicted injury.[2] However, a contemporary reviewer interpreted his tears as those of rage rather than pain:

> There is something very characteristic in the little boy (who has cut his finger) grasping the knife, with obstinacy that defies remonstrance, and crying with extreme passion, - not from any pain at his wound, but at the attempt of the maid to wrest the knife from his hand. - The character of the boy is truly that of a little <u>John Bull</u>.[3]

Such extreme expressions were regarded at the time as a good test of the painter's skill. In the same Royal Academy exhibition of 1809, Thomas Heaphy showed a watercolour, *The Village Doctress* (fig.23), which has a very similar subject. It seems to have been quite common at this period for genre painters to vie with one another to paint difficult themes, and it is not clear whether Heaphy was emulating Wilkie, or *vice versa* (Wilkie recorded his admiration for Heaphy in his journal in 1810 - see cat.27)

Boys with toy boats are a common motif in genre painting, and may well be intended to signify a taste for seafaring as an element in British national identity. The most famous example is Turner's group of boys in the foreground of *Dido Building Carthage* (1815: National Gallery).

1. Deuchar, *op.cit.*, p.9.

2. A. Cunningham, *The Life of Sir David Wilkie*, London: John Murray, 1843, Vol I, pp.218-9.

3. *Bell's Weekly Messenger*, 21 May 1809.

47. Distraining for Rent (1815) (page 51)

SIR DAVID WILKIE (1785-1841)
Signed and dated 1815
Oil on panel
81.3 x 123 cm.

Provenance: Bought by the Directors of the British Institution for 600 guineas, 1817; Abraham Raimbach; William Wells, Redleaf; Christie's 12 May 1848 (lot 74, bought in); Christie's 10th May 1890 (lot 81), bt. Agnew; Samuel Cunliffe-Lister, later 1st Lord Masham, thence by descent; purchased by National Gallery of Scotland from sale of pictures by Trustees of Swinton Settled Estates, 1975.
First exhibited: Royal Academy, 1815 (no.118).
Literature: L.Errington, *Tribute to Wilkie*, Edinburgh: National Galleries of Scotland, 1985, pp.60-69; D.Macmillan, *Painting in Scotland: the Golden Age*, Oxford: Phaidon Press, 1986, pp.166-7.
Engraved: by Abraham Raimbach, 1828.
National Gallery of Scotland
(Nottingham only)

The similarities of this painting to Greuze's *L'Accordée de Village*, and its reception in 1815, have been discussed in the Introduction, pp.15 and 25. The subject is a farmer who has been unable to pay his rent: the bailiffs take an inventory of his possessions, while the neighbours protest on his behalf; even the baby's cradle and the spinning wheel are set out ready to be taken away.

47

Distraining for Rent raises genre to the level of history painting, focussing on pathos rather than on the condescending comedy of some of Wilkie's earlier paintings. His success in conveying the emotional states of the main characters was much appreciated by contemporary critics. The critic of *The Examiner* said the father had "the involuntary attitude and look of a person pierced to the heart by some sudden and dire evil. It is that ponderous depression of spirits in which the body bendingly sympathises; the eyes are directed downwards; the complexion is dimmed; the head rests on the hand." He is unable even to respond to the small boy who tugs at his coat - a contrast to the usual kindly paternal feeling shown by rustic fathers in paintings. The group of neighbours, meanwhile, exhibit "a roused phrenzy of action and passion. The Bailiff's pauperising business has stimulated their friendly rage. This is glowingly painted in their fiery eyes and complexions, their clenched hands, and hostile advance, which is checked by the prudential arm of a shoemaker."[1] This was a liberal paper, and the writer was probably Robert Hunt, a friend of Wilkie's. His appreciation of the group of neighbours is significant; for other observers it could have been a worrying reminder of popular disturbances. Hunt points out that the bailiff "grasps the club-stick for his defence"; and shoemakers were traditionally associated with radical politics.

More conservative critics were disturbed by the painting (see p.25). Cunningham, in his *Life*, tried to explain the distraining as a consequence of the farmer's inefficiency: "the idle jack, the burnt-out fire, the empty bee-hive, are so many intimations of mismanagement or slackness of industry."[2] However, these details are very difficult to discern in the painting. The "idle jack" may be the spinning-wheel, but it is idle because it is being used to pay debts, not because the farmer's wife is lazy; the fire may be burnt

out, but the windows are open so it is presumably a warm day; the empty bee-hive, hanging above the bed, is hardly conspicuous. It seems much more likely that Wilkie meant the observer to sympathise with the farmer, rather than to condemn him - in which case there was, as Beaumont and other critics noted, implied criticism of the hard-hearted landlord.

In 1832, when Douglas Jerrold presented a *tableau vivant* based on the painting for his play, *The Rent Day*, he certainly intended a radical political meaning. Wilkie went to see the play and expressed his approval, asking Clarkson Stanfield to pass on his thanks to Jerrold, "whose inventive fancy has created out of the dumb show of a picture all the living characters and progressive events of real life".[3] Jerrold's probable opinion of the ability of painting to criticise the rich and help the poor is quoted at the head of Chapter Four of the Introduction (p.23).

1. *The Examiner*, Sunday 4 June 1815, p.365.
2. A. Cunningham, *The Life of Sir David Wilkie*, London, 1843, Vol I, p.435.
3. See M.Meisel *Realizations: Narrative, Pictorial and Theatrical Arts in Nineteenth-century England*, Princeton: Princeton University Press, 1983, p.142 and 165. A copy of Wilkie's letter to Stanfield was pasted on the back of the panel and is now in the archives of the National Gallery of Scotland.

48. The Penny Wedding (1818) *(page 52)*

SIR DAVID WILKIE (1785-1841)
Signed and dated 1818.
Oil on panel
64.4 x 95.6 cm.
Provenance: Commissioned from the artist by the Prince Regent (later George IV), who paid £525 for the painting and £20 for the frame.
First exhibited: Royal Academy 1819 (no.153).
Literature: Oliver Millar, *The Later Georgian Pictures in the Collection of Her Majesty the Queen*, London: Phaidon, 1969, no. 1176; Lindsay Errington, *Tribute to Wilkie*, Edinburgh: National Galleries of Scotland, 1985, pp.13-23; H.A.D. Miles et al., *Sir David Wilkie of Scotland*, Raleigh: North Carolina Museum of Art, 1987, cat. 18; Duncan Macmillan, *Painting in Scotland: the Golden Age*, Oxford: Phaidon Press, 1986, p.171.
Engraved: by James Stewart, 1832; and by Greatbach.
Lent by Her Majesty the Queen

The composition, characterisation and narrative of this painting have been discussed in detail in the Introduction, pp.8-9.

49

The Prince Regent commissioned a painting from Wilkie as a companion to *Blind Man's Buff*, but left the choice of subject up to the artist. Wilkie described it in the Academy catalogue: "This is a marriage festival, once common in Scotland, at which each of the guests paid a subscription to defray the expenses of the feast, and by the overplus to enable the new-married couple to commence housekeeping." Wilkie acknowledged, therefore, that his scene was set in the past. As Lindsay Errington has shown, Wilkie was drawing on a number of recent Scottish literary and artistic representations of penny weddings, and chose to convey a decorous and nostalgic view of the custom, glossing over the drunkenness and licentiousness which had led to its suppression. His characters are in late eighteenth-century dress, and the musicians are based on portraits of Niel and Donald Gow, celebrated figures of an earlier generation.

David Allan, an earlier Scottish painter whom Wilkie admired greatly, had painted a watercolour, *The Penny Wedding*, in 1795 (National Galleries of Scotland). Duncan Macmillan points out that Allan's social view was "touched by Rousseau", whereas Wilkie's version, with its prominent gentry, reflects Sir Walter Scott's nostalgic vision of a harmonious paternalistic society.[1] Alexander Carse exhibited an oil painting, *A Penny Wedding*[2] in the same year as Wilkie. However, his version of the subject looks self-consciously rustic, with the faces of the characters verging on caricature, in contrast to Wilkie's elegant and graceful figures.

1. D.Macmillan, *op. cit.*, p.73.
2. Private collection, on loan to the National Gallery of Scotland.

49. The Cotter's Saturday Night (1832-7)
(page 51)

SIR DAVID WILKIE (1785-1841)
Oil on panel
83.8 x 108 cm.
Provenance: Painted for Francis G.Moon ?1832-7; Francis G.Moon sale, Christie's 12 April 1872, lot 191, bt. Maclean; sold Christie's 25 May 1897, lot 90, bt. J.N.May; sold Christie's 4 April 1928, lot 60, bt. ?Brown; Luke Parsons, from whom purchased for the Gallery by Hamilton Trustees, 1948.
First exhibited: Royal Academy 1837 (no.358). "The cheerfu' supper done, wi' serious face, etc." - Burns.
Literature: D.Macmillan, *Painting in Scotland: the Golden Age*, Oxford: Phaidon Press, 1986, pp.175-181.
Glasgow Museums: Art Gallery and Museum, Kelvingrove

This painting illustrates Robert Burns' poem, *The Cotter's Saturday Night*, specifically the scene towards the end where the family gather round to listen while the father reads the Bible:

> The cheerfu' supper done, wi' serious face
> They round the ingle form a circle wide;
> The sire turns o'er, wi' patriarchal grace,
> The big ha'-bible, ance his father's pride...
> (ll.100-104)

Wilkie follows the poem faithfully in some respects, notably in his depiction of blushing Jenny, the eldest daughter, and her bashful suitor who gazes at her from the shadows. However, he adds the grandmother, who is not mentioned in the poem, thus emphasizing the connection between religious faith and filial affection.

Duncan Macmillan has shown that this painting reflects the ideas of Thomas Chalmers, whom Wilkie knew and admired. Chalmers had upheld the right of Scottish congregations to choose their own ministers; Wilkie, a minister's son himself, represents the cotter and his family as people quite capable of managing their own religious affairs. The lighting, the canopy over Jenny's head, and the Madonna-like mother and child, all add to the sacramental mood of the picture.

The style of the painting is typical of Wilkie's later work, in which rich glazes and subtle chiaroscuro take over from the fine detail of his earlier work. Its artistic sources are no longer Teniers and the genre painters, but seventeenth-century religious painters: Rembrandt, Georges de la Tour, the Dutch followers of Caravaggio. The refined beauty of the figures, whose faces and hands (hardly those of hard-working cotters) are picked out by the candlelight, also reflects these sources.

Many nineteenth-century painters depicted Burns' poem, or selected lines from it (see cats.13,14,16 in this exhibition). Its themes of piety, modesty, respect and family affection had a very wide appeal. Indeed, in 1863 a critic claimed that its significance was universal:

> Burns was a genius wide as nature; and his verses, even when the dialect be of Scotland, are as universal as our common humanity. They come home, indeed, to every heart, just because in all times and in every country the human breast throbs with the same master emotions. "The Cotter's Saturday Night" is as essentially true to the labourers of Hampshire as to the peasantry of Argyll.[1]

In actual fact, *The Cotter's Saturday Night* is one of Burns' more accessible poems, with several verses written in standard English, and expressing unusually conservative political sentiments.

1. *Art Journal*, 1863, p.112.

50

50. Studies for "The Penny Wedding" (1818)

SIR DAVID WILKIE (1785-1841)
Signed.
Pen and brown ink on paper
24.7 x 19.2 cm.
Provenance: P.M.Turner; purchased 1942.
Literature: D.B.Brown, *Sir David Wilkie: Drawings and Sketches in the Ashmolean Museum*, Oxford: Morton Morris & Co in association with the Ashmolean Museum, 1985, cat.9.
The Visitors of the Ashmolean Museum, Oxford

The sequence of drawings for *The Penny Wedding* (cats.50,51,52) illustrates Wilkie's method of working at this period of his career. Small, rapidly executed pen sketches were used to fix the elements of the composition and achieve fluency in the relationship of the figures to one another. Then Wilkie would move on to careful studies of individual figures, made from posed models (cat.51). On this sheet, most of the drawings are concerned with the group on the left of the final painting, the couple who provide amusement for the girl and old woman to either side of them (see Introduction, p.8-9).

51

51. Study of a Man and a Woman: Study for "The Penny Wedding" (1818)

SIR DAVID WILKIE (1785-1841)
Signed
Black and red chalks over pencil on paper
22.1 x 16.5 cm.
Provenance: Hugh Walpole; purchased 1952.
Literature: D.B.Brown, *Sir David Wilkie: Drawings and Sketches in the Ashmolean Museum*, Oxford: Morton Morris & Co in association with the Ashmolean Museum, 1985, cat.10.
The Visitors of the Ashmolean Museum, Oxford

See cat. 50. This is a drawing for the couple on the left: the man is eager, the woman feigns indifference and looks away; the implication is that they will be the next to wed. Comparison with the final painting shows that Wilkie made further changes to the group, altering the position of the woman's arm and changing her expression.

52. Sketch for The Penny Wedding (1817)

(page 52)

SIR DAVID WILKIE (1785-1841)
Watercolour on paper
Signed and dated 1817
12 x 19.7 cm.
Provenance: Collection of Sir William Knighton; given to the museum by Charles Fairfax Murray, 1912.
Literature: L.Errington, "The Genre Paintings of Wilkie" in H.A.D. Miles et al., *Sir David Wilkie of Scotland*, Raleigh: North Carolina Museum of Art, 1986, p.13.
Lent by the Syndics of the Fitzwilliam Museum, Cambridge

This would seem to represent an early idea for *The Penny Wedding*. At this stage the incident on the left has already been envisaged: the woman is reluctant to rise and dance with her partner, while her companions encourage her, an idea that is expressed with greater subtlety in the final painting. As the composition was refined, the groups became more harmonious, and narrative clarity was increased (in this watercolour it is not even clear who are the bride and groom), although it could be argued that the final effect is more contrived than in this charmingly natural-looking watercolour.

52

53

53. Study for "Distraining for Rent"

SIR DAVID WILKIE (1785-1841)
Signed
Pencil and watercolour on paper
11.7 x 19 cm.
Provenance: presented to the museum by
F.F.Madan, 1938.
Literature: D.B.Brown, *Sir David Wilkie: Drawings and Sketches in the Ashmolean Museum*, Oxford: Morton Morris & Co in association with the Ashmolean Museum, 1985, cat.3.
The Visitors of the Ashmolean Museum, Oxford

If this is a study for *Distraining for Rent* (cat.47), then it seems that at one stage Wilkie thought of showing the bailiffs actually dragging away the family's bedding, a motif that would have made the painting much more dramatic and violent.

54. The Blind Fiddler (1811)

JOHN BURNET (1784-1868)
after SIR DAVID WILKIE (1785-1841)
Engraving
48 x 55.1 cm.

Provenance: not known (entered museum in 1839).
The British Museum

The painting on which this print is based (fig.1) entered the National Gallery in 1826 and thus became one of Wilkie's most famous and influential works. It combined two themes which were to be of great importance for nineteenth-century rustic genre painters: the happy cottage family, and the charity of the poor towards their own class. The painting was commissioned by Sir George Beaumont, who made efforts, which were resisted by Wilkie, to encourage contacts between the painter and the poet, William Wordsworth. Wordsworth wrote a poem, *The Power of Music*, about the same blind fiddler depicted by Wilkie, describing the reaction to his playing of passers-by in the street. When Joseph Farington went to see the picture in Beaumont's house in November 1806, he was entertained by Lady Beaumont's readings from Wordsworth and from Robert Burns after tea.[1]

The inscription on the print gives more prominence to the patron of the painting than the artist: it is dedicated "to Sir George Beaumont Bart, whose Superior Judgment and Liberality, have led him to appreciate, and encourage early and extraordinary merit." Beaumont's crest and motto, *erectus non elatus* are also inscribed on the print.

Like the poetry of Wordsworth and Burns, the painting and print celebrate the enjoyments of the poor and their sensitivity to music. People from a humble background are shown as capable of complex emotions, which were described in detail by contemporary reviewers (see Introduction, p.23). The engraver has made efforts to transcribe these complex emotions faithfully, although he falls far short of the original in this respect. Abraham Raimbach was to be more successful in preserving the subtle psychology of Wilkie's work in the transition from painting to print (fig.20).

The presence of prints after Wilkie's paintings in America meant that his compositions were made use of by American genre painters. Eastman Johnson, for example, adapted the idea of *The Blind Fiddler* for his painting, *Fiddling his Way*, in which the fiddler is black (fig.24).

1. K.Cave, ed., *The Diary of Joseph Farington, R.A.*, New Haven and London: Yale University Press, 1982, Vol. VIII, p.2898, 7 November 1806.

54

Fig.24 Eastman Johnson, *Fiddling his Way*, 1866. Oil on Canvas, 61.5 x 92 cm.
The Chrysler Museum of Art, Norfolk, VA. Bequest of Walter P. Chrysler, Jr, 89.60.

BIBLIOGRAPHY

Anon., *The Wilkie Gallery. A Selection of the Best Pictures of the Late Sir David Wilkie, R.A.*, London: George Virtue, 1851.

Anderson, G.-N., and J.Wright, *The Pursuit of Leisure: Victorian Depictions of Pastimes*, Nottingham: Djanogly Art Gallery in association with Lund Humphries, 1997.

The Art Journal, 1849-.

The Athenaeum, 1850-.

Barrell, J., *The Dark Side of the Landscape: the Rural Poor in English Painting, 1730-1840*, Cambridge: Cambridge University Press, 1980.

Bayard, J., *Works of Splendour and Imagination: the Exhibition Watercolour, 1770-1870*, New Haven: Yale Center for British Art, 1981.

Bell's Weekly Messenger, 1809-.

Bermingham, A., *Landscape and Ideology: the English Rustic Tradition, 1740-1860*, London and Berkeley: University of California Press, 1986.

Blunt, Revd. J.J., *The Duties of a Parish Priest*, London: John Murray, 1856.

Bowles, M., *Characters and Incidents of Village Life, mostly founded on fact; intended for the religious and moral instruction of the poor*, London: C.J.G. and F.Rivington, 1831.

Brettell, R.B. and C.B., *Painters and the Peasant in the Nineteenth Century*, New York: Rizzoli, 1983.

Brookner, A., *Greuze: the Rise and Fall of an Eighteenth-Century Phenomenon*, London: Paul Elek, 1972.

Brown, C., *Scenes of Everyday Life: Dutch Genre Painting of the Seventeenth Century*, London: Faber and Faber, 1984.

Brown, D.B., *Sir David Wilkie: Drawings and Sketches in the Ashmolean Museum*, Oxford: Morton Morris & Co. in association with the Ashmolean Museum, 1985.

Brown, F.K., *Fathers of the Victorians: the Age of Wilberforce*, Cambridge: Cambridge University Press, 1961.

Butler, M., *Romantics, Rebels and Reactionaries: English Literature and its Social Background, 1760-1830*, Oxford: Oxford University Press, 1981.

Casteras, S., "Oh! Emigration! thou'rt the curse...Victorian Images of Emigration Themes", *Journal of Pre-Raphaelite Studies*, Vol. VI, no.1, November 1985, pp.1-23.

Casteras, S., and R.Parkinson (eds.), *Richard Redgrave, 1804-1888*, New Haven and London: Yale University Press, in association with the Victoria and Albert Museum and the Yale Center for British Art, 1988.

Cave, K. (ed.), *The Diary of Joseph Farington*, Vol. VIII, July 1806-December 1807, New Haven and London: Yale University Press, 1982.

Cherry, D., "The Hogarth Club: 1858-1861", *Burlington Magazine*, no. 122, April 1980, pp.237-244.

Cherry, D. *Painting Women: Victorian Women Artists*, London and New York: Routledge, 1993.

Coats, A.W. (ed.), *Poverty in the Victorian Age, Vol III: Charity, 1815-70*, Farnborough: Gregg International, 1973.

Collins, W., *Memoirs of the Life of William Collins, Esq., R.A.*, 2 vols., Wakefield: E.P.Publishing, 1978 (first published 1848).

Cook, E.T., and A.Wedderburn (eds.), *The Works of John Ruskin*, 39 vols., London: George Allen, 1903-12.

Cope, C.W., *Reminiscences of Charles West Cope, R.A.*, London: Richard Bentley & Son, 1891.

Crow, T., *Painters and Public Life in Eighteenth-Century Paris*, New Haven and London: Yale University Press, 1985.

Cullen, F., *Visual Politics: the Representation of Ireland, 1750-1930*, Cork: Cork University Press, 1997.

Cunningham, A., *The Life of Sir David Wilkie*, 3 vols., London: John Murray, 1843.

De Selincourt, E. (ed.), *The Poetical Works of William Wordsworth*, 5 Vols., Oxford: Clarendon Press, 1940-9.

Deuchar, S., *Paintings, Politics and Porter: Samuel Whitbread II (1764-1815) and British Art*, London: Whitbread & Co. for the Museum of London, 1984.

Dowling, L., *The Vulgarization of Art: the Victorians and Aesthetic Democracy*, Charlottesville and London: University Press of Virginia, 1996.

Dunbabin, J., *Rural Discontent in nineteenth-century Britain*, London: Faber, 1974.

Eliot, G., *Adam Bede*, (first published 1859) London: Zodiac Press, 1978.

Eliot, G., *Middlemarch*, (first published 1872) London: Zodiac Press, 1967.

Errington, L., *Masterclass: Robert Scott Lauder and his Pupils*, Edinburgh: National Gallery of Scotland, 1983.

Errington, L., *Social and Religious Themes in English Art, 1840-1860*, New York and London: Garland Publishing, 1984.

Errington, L., *Tribute to Wilkie*, Edinburgh: National Galleries of Scotland, 1985.

Errington, L., *Alexander Carse, c.1770-1843*, Edinburgh: National Galleries of Scotland, 1987.

The Examiner, 1808-.

Fox, C., and F.Greenacre, *Painting in Newlyn, 1880-1930*, London: Barbican Art Gallery, 1985.

Gear, J., *Masters or Servants? A Study of Selected English Painters and their Patrons of the late Eighteenth and early Nineteenth Centuries*, New York and London: Garland Publishing, Inc., 1977.

Gibson, A., and J. Forbes White, *George Paul Chalmers, R.S.A.*, Edinburgh: David Douglas, 1879.

Greg, A., *The Cranbrook Colony*, Wolverhampton: Wolverhampton Art Gallery, 1977.

Hamlyn, R., *Robert Vernon's Gift: British Art for the Nation, 1847*, London: Tate Gallery, 1993.

Harrison, B., "Philanthropy and the Victorians", *Victorian Studies*, IX, 1966, pp.353-74.

Healey, E., *Lady Unknown: the Life of Angela Burdett-Coutts*, London: Sidgwick and Jackson, 1978.

Heleniak, K., *William Mulready*, New Haven and London: Yale University Press, 1980.

Hemingway, A., *Landscape Imagery and Urban Culture in Early Nineteenth-century Britain*, Cambridge: Cambridge University Press, 1992.

Hewitt, M., "District Visiting and the Construction of Domestic Space in the Mid-Nineteenth Century", in I.Bryden and J.Floyd, eds., *Reading the Nineteenth-century Domestic Space*, Manchester: Manchester University Press, forthcoming 1998.

Hobsbawm, E.J., and G.Rudé, *Captain Swing*, London: Lawrence and Wishart, 1969.

Hone, W., *The Every-day Book, or Everlasting Calendar of Popular Amusements*, 2 vols, London: Hunt and Clarke, 1826.

Houghton, W.E., *The Victorian Frame of Mind, 1830-1870*, New Haven and London: Yale University for Wellesley College, 1957.

Howitt, W., *The Book of the Seasons; or the Calendar of Nature*, 2nd ed., London: Richard Bentley, 1833.

Howitt, W., "Cottage Life", in A.A.Watts, ed., *The Cabinet of Modern Art, and Literary Souvenir*, 1837, pp.67-79.

Howkins, A., *Reshaping Rural England: a Social History, 1850-1925*, London: Harper Collins, 1991.

Hume, D., *Enquiries Concerning Human Understanding and Concerning the Principles of Morals*, Oxford: Clarendon Press, 1989 (first pub. 1777).

Inglis, K.S., *Churches and the Working Classes in Victorian England*, London: Routledge and Kegan Paul, 1963.

Irving, W., *The Sketch Book of Geoffrey Crayon, Gent.*, London: John Murray, 1820.

Johns, E., *American Genre Painting: the Politics of Everyday Life*, New Haven and London: Yale University Press, 1991.

Johnson, E.D.H., *Painters of the British Social Scene from Hogarth to Sickert*, London: Weidenfeld and Nicolson, 1986.

King, L. Saunders, *The Industrialization of Taste: Victorian England and the Art Union of London*, Ann Arbor, Michigan: UMI Research Press, 1985.

Kinsley, J. (ed.), *The Poems and Songs of Robert Burns*, 3 Vols., Oxford: Clarendon Press, 1968.

Kitson Clark, G., *Churchmen and the Condition of England: 1832-1885*, London: Methuen, 1973.

Kriz, K.D., "An English Arcadia Revisited and Reassessed: Holman Hunt's *The Hireling Shepherd* and the Rural Tradition", *Art History*, Vol. 10, no.4, December 1987, pp.475-91.

The Literary Gazette, 1837.

Lloyd Williams, J., *Dutch Art and Scotland: a Reflection of Taste*, Edinburgh: National Gallery of Scotland, 1992.

McKerrow, M., *The Faeds: a Biography*, Edinburgh: Canongate, 1982.

Macleod, D.S., *Art and the Victorian Middle Class: Money and the Making of Cultural Identity*, Cambridge: Cambridge University Press, 1996.

Macmillan, D., *Painting in Scotland: the Golden Age*, Oxford: Phaidon Press, 1986.

Maidment, B., *Reading Popular Prints, 1790-1870*, Manchester: Manchester University Press, 1996.

Marks, A.S., "The Paintings of David Wilkie to 1825", PhD diss., Courtauld Institute of Art, University of London, 1968.

Marks, A.S., "Rivalry at the Royal Academy: Wilkie, Turner and Bird", *Studies in Romanticism*, Vol. 20, no. 3, Fall 1981, pp.333-62.

Meisel, M., *Realizations: Narrative, Pictorial, and Theatrical Arts in Nineteenth-century England*, Princeton: Princeton University Press, 1983.

Melvill, H., *Sermons*, London: Rivingtons, 1870.

Miles, H.A.D., and D.B.Brown (with contributions by Sir Ivor Batchelor, Lindsay Errington and Arthur S.Marks), *Sir David Wilkie of Scotland*, Raleigh: North Carolina Museum of Art, 1987.

Miles, H., *Sir David Wilkie*, London: Richard L.Feigen and Company, 1994.

Millar, O., *The Later Georgian Pictures in the Collection of Her Majesty the Queen*, London: Phaidon, 1969.

Mingay, G.E., *Rural Life in Victorian England*, London: Heinemann, 1977.

Mingay, G.E. (ed.), *The Victorian Countryside: Image and Reality*, 2 vols, London: Routledge and Kegan Paul, 1981.

The Morning Post, 1807-.

Mount, H., "The Reception of Dutch Genre Painting in England, 1695-1829", PhD diss., University of Cambridge, 1991.

Nead, L., *Myths of Sexuality: Representations of Women in Victorian Britain*, Oxford: Basil Blackwell, 1988.

Ormond, R., *Sir Edwin Landseer*, London: Thames and Hudson in association with Philadelphia Museum of Art and the Tate Gallery, 1981.

Owen, D., *English Philanthropy, 1660-1960*, Oxford: Oxford University Press, 1965.

Owen, F., and D.B.Brown, *Collector of Genius: a Life of Sir George Beaumont*, New Haven and London: Yale University Press, 1988.

Parkinson, R., *Catalogue of British Oil Paintings, 1820-1860*, London: Victoria and Albert Museum, 1990.

Parris, L. (ed.), *Pre-Raphaelite Papers*, London: Tate Gallery, 1984.

Paulson, R., *Hogarth: His Life, Art and Times*, 3 Vols., Cambridge: Lutterworth Press, 1992.